FROM FASHION TO POLITICS:

HADASSAH AND JEWISH AMERICAN WOMEN IN THE POST WORLD WAR II ERA

SHIRLI BRAUTBAR

ACADEMIC
STUDIES
PRESS

FROM FASHION TO POLITICS

HADASSAH AND JEWISH AMERICAN WOMEN

IN THE POST WORLD WAR II ERA

———————— SHIRLI BRAUTBAR ————————

Boston
2013

Library of Congress Cataloging-in-Publication Data:
A bibliographic record for this title is available from the Library of Congress

ISBN 978-1-61811-159-3 (hardback)

ISBN 978-1-611811-295-8 (paperback

Book design by Olga Grabovsky
On the cover: Photographs courtesy of Hadassah

Published by Academic Studies Press in 2012, paperback edition 2013.
28 Montfern Avenue
Brighton, MA 02135, USA
press@academicstudiespress.com
www.academicstudiespress.com

CONTENTS

LIST OF ILLUSTRATIONS

ACKNOWLEDGMENTS

As with most academic works, this book could not have been written without tremendous support. Several years ago as a graduate student at the University of Southern California, I asked myself the question: is Hadassah history important? I did not anticipate finding that Hadassah played such a central role in American Jewish history. I would like to thank the University of Southern California's History Department for supporting my early scholastic devolvement both financially and otherwise. In addition, the Graduate School at the University of Southern California granted several fellowships that supported my research. I am especially thankful to my advisor, Lois Banner, at the University of Southern California History Department for her unwavering support and guidance throughout the years. I would also like to thank David Kaufman at Hofstra University for his advice and guidance and Carla Kaplan in the English Department of the University of Southern California for her input. The Casden Center for the Study of Jewish Life in America under the directorship of Professor Barry Glassner also provided me generous support in the form of the Winnick Family Fellowship.

Susan Woodland, former director of the Hadassah Archive at the Center for Jewish History in New York, truly deserves the greatest thanks and respect for all that she has done for me and other Jewish scholars. She is a credit to her profession, having organized the collection in such a way that it is easily managed by scholars. More importantly, she took the time to assist me on this project every step of the way. In addition, I also utilized the archives at the Philadelphia Historical Society, the Bremen institute, and the Library of Congress and would like to thank all the archivists at those collections that helped along the way. Andrea Lieber at Dickinson College deserves thanks as well.

For the past five years, I have found my academic home at Nevada State College as a history professor. Nevada State College has truly become my home away from home, and the friendships and support that I have received from my colleagues and administration have been extraordinary. I would like to thank Andy Kuniyuki for his support and for hours of enlightening conversation about religion and the universe. Erika Beck has been there for support throughout this process. I would be remiss if I did not thank Angela Brommel for her personal and academic advice; she is a true friend. I also would like to acknowledge Gwen Sharp for her editorial eye, Kathy Damm for her advice, and Sally Helvesten Grey, editor of *Dress*, for all of her feedback on my work.

I begin my introduction writing about childhood memories, and that is fitting because I would not have the academic curiosity that I have today had my parents, Nachman and Ronit, not raised me to always ask questions and to revere learning. Most of all, my husband, Pete La Chapelle, has served as editor and cheerleader for the years it has taken to write this book. I have been blessed to have found my *beshert*. I would also like to thank Sigalit Klien, Jacques Brautbar, and Ilana Fisher for their support throughout the years. I dedicate this book to my children, Asher and Samuel, with the hopes that they grow to be men who appreciate their Jewish heritage and always respect the women in their lives.

INTRODUCTION

My earliest memory of life in America is of my older sister wading in a pool under the California sunshine and talking about missing home. Home, at that time, meant Israel. *Yaradnu*—the Hebrew term for leaving Israel—actually translates as "we went down." In the Jewish imagination, one can only "go down" from a place as holy as Israel. Two years before, we had left Israel and immigrated to the United States so that my father could pursue his career. At the time, I remember having difficulties adjusting to life in America and missing my grandparents and aunts, all of whom still lived in Israel. I grew up in a family dedicated to Zionism—making my connection to Israel predetermined. I attended a Jewish day school. Surrounded by American-born Jews, I observed as they struggled to understand the place of Israel in their lives.

Like me, they too had to contend with the tenuous position of being both American and having an Israeli heritage. Mine was and is a slow unfolding process of negotiation. However, I noticed extreme reactions among many of my peers. Some embraced the concept of Israel so wholeheartedly that they neglected to notice the reality of the existing Israeli people and nation. Others detested what they felt was a phony and forced connection to a Jewish state that seemed not only foreign but also politically problematic.

My interest in Zionism has existed all my life, and my work as a historian reflects my personal questions about the negotiation of Jewish identity, especially the issue of Zionism. Melding interests in women's history and Zionism, this book is a historical study of the most powerful women's Zionist organization in history and arguably one of the most influential Jewish organizations in the world—Hadassah.

The balancing of Jewishness and Zionist identity is a relatively new phenomenon in Jewish life. For the most part, it is a by-product of the modern era with its revolutionary emphasis on nationalism and rights. The question of how Zionism — at one time a marginal political ideology — evolved into a dominant component of Jewish identity can be answered by looking at groups like Hadassah. In this case, Zionism galvanized a pool of Jewish women waiting for the opportunity to contribute to Jewish causes. That marriage of ideology and activity was transmitted through Hadassah to its over 300,000 members in the 1950s and 1960s, and through them to their husbands and children. Through Hadassah membership, generations of Jewish women and their families adopted Zionism as a central aspect of American Jewish identity.

Simultaneously, the role of women within American and Jewish culture was redefined through the participation of women en masse in Hadassah. As this book will show, messages about Jewish identity were woven with empowering and sometimes contradictory gender ideals. Although often portrayed in the literature and the public imagination as a women's social club of "ladies that lunch," the organization's lobbying activity and philanthropic work often served explicitly political purposes and carried important political repercussions, even influencing the shifting geopolitical realities of the Cold War. By engaging over 300,000 American Jewish women in the 1950s and 1960s in a campaign to support the nascent state of Israel, Hadassah members forged a Jewish women's political consciousness focused on the Jewish state while simultaneously constructing an American Jewish women's identity based on political and social action.

This book explores how Jewish American women used Hadassah during the post–World War II era as a site to fashion a new vision of women's roles within the Jewish community and to create a place for women's participation within Jewish political and philanthropic culture. Hadassah proved to be a central actor in the shaping of policy in both Israel and the United States. It provided an avenue for women to be active participants in the formation of a Jewish identity based not solely on religion or culture but on the pursuit of political goals and humanitarian aid. I argue that while confronting various social, cultural, and political forces, these women challenged traditional social and gender roles. In doing so, they combined their own sense of identity as women with important new notions of Jewish identity and community that became a model for Jewish American society as a whole as the post–World War II era progressed. While social activities, such as fashion shows, and networking played a part in Hadassah, these endeavors often served other purposes; they challenged commonly held notions about women's and Jewish identities.

Hadassah activism and ideology evolved during the 1950s and 1960s, responding to shifting historical trends. This book addresses four major themes: gender norms and Hadassah's role in women's empowerment or disempowerment; Hadassah's rhetoric on both domestic and foreign policy issues during the Cold War; Hadassah's civil rights and other domestic policy campaigns; and, finally, images and policies relating to Arabs in Hadassah discourse. The formation of Jewish American women's identities and the evolving political, cultural, and social ramifications undergird all these themes. While identities are constructed by the interactions of individual psychology with social and cultural norms, they are also inscribed through actions or, as Judith Butler argues, "performances" that seek to maintain or reinvent identities. I seek to understand the ways in which Hadassah articulated a discourse on identity and how the organization applied itself in the public sphere.[1]

Hadassah provided Jewish middle- and upper-class women with an outlet for fulfilling political, spiritual, and educational aspirations and encouraged women to engage in political, civic, and communal development. At the same time, Hadassah rhetoric and activities often utilized hegemonic gender ideals of domesticity and feminine consumer practices, such as fashion, to legitimate the participation of women in the nontraditional sphere of public action and education. The post–World War II era saw significant changes in women's history, and Hadassah's gendered language changed over time, accommodating popular trends while at the same time contesting gender roles.

Hadassah's negotiation with Cold War rhetoric and policy also reflected complexities and contradictions: the organization both championed Cold War rhetoric on foreign policy issues and combated

McCarthyism's assault on civil liberties. Civil rights constituted one arena where Hadassah policy and rhetoric presented a unified stance, locating the significance of civil rights activism in both American culture and Jewish circles.

Through Hadassah pamphlets, newsletters, conventions, and fashion shows, Hadassah engaged in other domestic policy issues as well. It strongly urged women to exercise their right to vote while presenting a decidedly progressive and liberal stance on domestic issues. On foreign policy, however, Hadassah took a conservative approach and championed hard-line anti-Soviet Cold War rhetoric in order to emphasize the importance of Israel to the West and to democracy. The most conflicted aspect of Hadassah ideology centered around the changing images of, and policies concerning, Arabs and Arab states. On the one hand, Hadassah subscribed to an ideology of cultural pluralism and inclusion. Hadassah had always opened its medical and social programs to Arabs in Israel and beyond. However, Hadassah rhetoric also increasingly positioned Arab nations as a threat to both the survival of Israel and democracy.

The roots of the national organization stemmed from a small Hadassah chapter of the Daughters of Zion, a group created by the Federation of American Zionists to garner more women members.[2] Once Henrietta Szold joined the group at the suggestion of Rabbi Judah Magnes, Hadassah shifted from a study circle to an activist group. By 1914, at the first national conference, 516 women were in attendance for the official naming of the organization as Hadassah: The Women's Zionist Organization of America.[3] It would become not only the most influential women's Zionist organization in America but also the largest Zionist membership organization in the world.[4] Hadassah women contributed to the development of an "emancipated" Jewish American woman whose purpose in life extended well beyond the confines of the domestic sphere into the arenas of fund-raising, politics, education, and women's social and cultural empowerment. Jewish cultural references served as the basic language from which Hadassah members built a new discourse on gender and culture that altered Jewish women's gender roles from an identity based solely on child rearing to one grounded in worldly pursuits. This process was complex. While challenging some aspects of the status quo, Hadassah members adopted many accepted gender roles in an effort to normalize their activities and place themselves within an accepted sphere of women's behavior.

Mira Katzburg-Yungman argues that Hadassah leaders made "no effort to encourage a feminist identity or feminist ideals that challenged the status quo."[5] While it is accurate that Hadassah leaders did not advocate the adoption of a particular feminist ideology or use the term *feminist*, the organization through its leadership, publications, and activities challenged traditional gender roles and provided American Jewish women with ways in which to contest hegemonic representations of women. A new field of literature is emerging by feminist and women's historians that seeks to broaden our understanding of feminism and the variety of paths toward feminist action.[6] In addition, Katzburg-Yungman argues that Hadassah was successful because of the fact that it aligned itself in an apolitical manner.[7] I contend that in certain ways Hadassah was apolitical in that it did not necessarily endorse a particular candidate or party; it did, however, lobby for explicitly political aims and worked to politicize a generation of American Jewish women.

During the post–World War II era, a period in American history that saw the rise of gender conservatism, Hadassah challenged the dominant ideology of domesticity. Hadassah took domestic ideology and turned it on its head by portraying motherhood as a political and cultural mandate. Hadassah women were "mothers" not only to their children but also to the Jewish people in America, to the emergent country of Israel, as well as to all Jewish children in general. Therefore, they were impelled to act politically on their children's behalf. During the 1950s and 1960s, Hadassah successfully reacted to new trends within the American social milieu and adapted them to its own purpose.

Although several works have explored the early years of Hadassah in the period between 1912 and 1935, I emphasize the era between the birth of Israel in the late 1940s and the major social shifts of the 1960s.[8] While Zionism in the postwar era garnered more acceptance in Jewish circles,[9] the establishment of the State of Israel in 1948 also brought about a shift in many American Zionist organizations. The initial purpose of Zionism — the establishment of a Jewish homeland in Palestine — had been accomplished. Hadassah, unlike many other Jewish organizations, had devoted much time to working in the *Yishuv*, the Jewish settlement in Palestine before the State of Israel was formed. Hadassah quickly adapted to a poststatehood world by channeling programs already in place in both America and Israel in new state-building directions.

Mary McCune provides a gender-focused account of Hadassah in its formative period. She argues that Hadassah members subscribed to a "gender consciousness" and actively challenged men and institutions that belittled their work.[10] June Sochen further analyzes the work of Hadassah in Palestine during the 1920s, and Naomi Lichtenberg has written a thorough analysis of Hadassah in the early period. She echoes McCune by establishing the political significance and gender challenges faced and successfully addressed by these founding members.[11] Yaffa Schlesinger analyzes Hadassah more from an organizational perspective, arguing that the effective Hadassah structure and the efficiency of its operation accounts for the successful growth of the organization.[12] Other scholars have also written about this early period.[13] Several biographical accounts of Hadassah matriarch Henrietta Szold also contribute to the historiography on Hadassah.[14] Michael Brown shows that Szold brought an Americanizing progressive sensibility to her work in Palestine that exposed Jews in Palestine and the emergent state to the language of American progressive principles.[15]

While interest in Hadassah during its early period is warranted, in 1925 Hadassah was a small but influential organization of 15,000 members. By the 1950s, it had exploded into a popular group numbering in the three hundred thousands.[16] In the 1990s, scholars of women's studies from within the field of Jewish studies called for the incorporation of Jewish women and gender studies into the historical narrative.[17] Much has been accomplished by scholars to more fully explore questions of women and Jewish history. Recently, a collection of essays addressing the Jewish women's experience of postwar America has highlighted the ways in which Jewish women uniquely responded to the challenges of that time.[18]

Postcolonial studies of nationalist movements have shown that while women may be absent from political narratives, gender often acts as a site of contestation of nationalist ideologies. Women's bodies often become symbols of the battle for nationalism, and women often bear the brunt of anxieties about imperialism. Postwar America represents a time in American history fraught with contradictions regarding gender roles, pushing women away from the "Rosie the Riveter" wartime appreciation of working women and pulling them into domestically bound notions of womanhood and then beginning to explode the myth of domestic tranquility in the 1960s. The decision to focus my narrative on the period from 1948 to 1970 was a deliberate one: this book seeks to understand how one of the largest groups representing Jewish women in American history contended with the waves of change surrounding them.

Historian Elaine Tyler May has shown how traditional gender roles and a Cold War mentality were inextricably linked and how they dominated the lives of white middle-class Protestant women during the 1950s.[19] I argue that while the Cold War did have an impact on the lives of members of Hadassah, they often manipulated Cold War hysteria to serve their own ends. On the one hand, they borrowed from Cold War rhetoric to support a pro-Israel stance; on the other hand, they opposed McCarthyism and blacklisting. In many ways, Hadassah serves as a case study for how a progressive organization wrestled with the pressures of the Cold War in America.

In postwar America, a barrage of messages about proper womanhood encouraged working women to return home. May shows how the domestic sphere became the sole focus for many middle-class Protestant housewives. Leila Rupp and Verta Taylor have argued that while the atmosphere restricted women's voices and confined women to the private sphere, women did attempt to challenge those gender norms through organizations aimed at furthering women's rights. This "elite sustained" movement of women working toward specifically feminist goals organized women in a time period often deemed as the "bleak and lonely years."[20] Women also engaged in other types of organizations and movements that sought to address issues not specifically related to advancing women's rights.

Social movements like the civil rights movement drew women's attention in this period; in addition, women joined organizations during the 1950s that, while not specifically women's rights groups, served to place women in the public sphere and often did address women's rights either directly or indirectly.[21] While Hadassah may not have been primarily a women's rights organization, it did provide women with a foray into the public and political realm. Often, Hadassah rhetoric and policy choices reflected a desire to improve women's status. Susan Levine, in her study of the American Association of University Women (AAUW) in the postwar era, contends:

> By most accounts, the women's movement died during the 1950s. Described by some as "the doldrums" and by others as an era in which the search for security after two decades of depression and war led American women to focus on family life to the exclusion of public concerns, the 1950s suggests the need for reevaluation of feminism's fate during that decade. Women's organizations neither disappeared nor remained silent about women's rights during the cold war years.[22]

The AAUW and other women's organizations actually grew in membership during the 1950s.[23] In her study, Levine finds that many women's organizations, faced with fears of anti-Communist rhetoric, shied away from challenging McCarthyism. In fact, Levine shows that some leaders in the AAUW backed McCarthyist ideology while others derided it, and the split in the organization on the issues of anti-Communism threatened to tear it apart with local chapters divided on the issues.[24]

Hadassah responded in a strikingly different way to the challenges of the Cold War assault on liberalism and feminism. Hadassah unequivocally denounced McCarthyism and worked to defend Americans' civil liberties; at the same time, however, Hadassah used anti-Communist rhetoric to argue that the United States should support Israel as a defender of democracy in an increasingly Communist-leaning Middle East. Civil rights was another area that Levine argues challenged many women's organizations in the Cold War era, and tensions over civil rights issues divided many women's organizations. A reexamination of civil rights policies and the pressure to admit blacks into the organizations also fragmented the AAUW.[25] Hadassah responded very differently, championing civil rights and encouraging its members to work toward desegregation. A Jewish organization, with a minute number of black American Jews, Hadassah never struggled with the question of inclusion of African Americans within its ranks.

Historians such as Lois Banner have detailed the development of a neo-Victorian regressive gender sensibility that appeared in the fifties within fashion and popular culture.[26] Yet Hadassah employed this sensibility in a manner that could be considered feminist. In offering women a site from which to contest dominant models of domesticity, Hadassah often emphasized popular notions of beauty and fashion; for example, they used activities like fashion shows to expand their membership. I address the debate centering on the questions of how women dealt with the images of domesticity and whether women really ascribed to those ideals or challenged them.[27] Some historians have viewed the postwar era as a time completely dominated by gender restrictions, while others contend that empowering messages about womanhood and the real-life experience of women challenged the restrictive images.[28] While Hadassah women adopted domestic notions and ideals, they also consciously used those ideals to challenge the very same messages.

Women's organizations have historically been a base from which women have entered the public sphere. As feminist theorists have argued, the "public sphere" has been both historically and academically defined as a space devoid of female actors. Participation in women's associations, according to Anne Firor Scott, "prepared women for politics, broadly defined."[29] Hadassah, in the postwar era, actively engaged women in both the political process and in the Jewish community building arena. In addition, as Scott points out, women as outsiders often recognized communal issues and problems that the male-dominated world neglected to recognize. Hadassah members often viewed the mission of Zionism and American public policy from a different perspective than Jewish American men might have. Hadassah focused not only on politics but also on practical applications to social welfare issues in America and Israel.

Like their Christian contemporaries, Jewish women during the early twentieth century started organizing. In 1893, the National Council of Jewish Women was formed. It was followed by Hadassah in 1912, synagogue sisterhoods in 1913, Pioneer Women, and Women's American ORT, to name a few. Joyce Antler has studied the Emma

Lazarus group, a small leftist organization of approximately 5,000 members. It had some similar goals to the more mainstream Hadassah such as civil rights, support of the United Nations Treaty on Genocide, and anti-McCarthyism activity.[30] Bnai Brith's women's group in 1947 had 90,000 members.[31] The NCJW, Hadassah's main rival, had 100,000 members at its height.[32] By the 1960s, Jewish women's organizations boasted nearly one million members, almost 20 percent of the American Jewish population and over 30 percent of that was Hadassah membership.[33] Jewish women's organizations in the United States shaped women's lives and identities as Jews, women, and Americans, and how that influenced over 300,000 Jewish women and their families sheds light on the experience of Jewish women in America.

Historians have analyzed the ways in which Jewish women merged their Jewishness with womanhood and American identity. Several general histories of the Jewish women's experience in America develop narratives of American Jewish history that not only include women but also often challenge the dominant paradigm accordingly.[34] Paula Hyman has shown that Jewish assimilation into American society shifted gender dynamics within the family, with men losing ground as the spiritual family caretakers and women assuming moral superiority in line with Victorian ideals about maternalism. Other studies have examined the Jewish women's immigrant experience in America from various angles, including consumption and labor activism.

A study of Hadassah in postwar America supports Arthur Goren's analysis that Jews in that time period participated in a "functional consensus" engaged in two primary public pursuits, "assuring Israel's security and striving for a liberal America (and by extension a liberal world order)."[35] Old World Liberalism, as Naomi Cohen defines it, was "the creed of individualism that sought to eradicate discrimination of the Old World."[36] Liberalism in America served the same function to preserve individualism, end discrimination, and ensure Jewish acceptance in America. Hadassah, like other Jewish groups and figures analyzed by Goren, defined Israel as a democratic bulwark against Communism and Arab aggression. The pursuit of liberal values had defined Hadassah's work from its inception but was more fully articulated during the postwar era through participation in civil rights and civil liberties activism and a variety of other policy stances that endorsed a liberal worldview. Alongside liberalism, Zionist organizations such as Hadassah adopted the ideology of cultural pluralism.[37] The one departure from the discourse on liberalism was a conflicted discourse on Arabs that vacillated between critical depictions and acceptance.

Henrietta Szold, described by renowned Zionist leader Louis Brandeis as "the Jewish Jane Addams," began her life as the daughter of Rabbi Benjamin Szold, living in Baltimore among a community of German Jews. Szold audited classes at the Jewish Theological Seminary and later became the literary secretary for the Jewish Publication Society and worked as the unofficial editor for the society until 1916.[38] In 1907, Szold joined an existing Daughters of Zion group in New York City already called the Hadassah Circle. In 1909, under the sponsorship of the Jewish Publication Society, Szold, accompanied by her mother, traveled to Palestine. After viewing firsthand the deplorable health conditions there, Szold returned to the United States with new inspiration. Szold's mother is said to have told Szold after seeing the lack of medical assistance available in Palestine, "This is what your group ought to do. What is the use of reading papers and arranging festivals? You should do practical work in Palestine."[39] By the end of 1912, Hadassah had accomplished its first goal by sending two nurses to Palestine via the new organization. Szold traveled to speak in various cities. By 1913, she established chapters in Philadelphia, Baltimore, Cleveland, Cincinnati, and Boston.[40]

By the post–World War II era, Hadassah sponsored Hadassah Medical Organization in Israel and a variety of social programs in Israel and in the United States, with an emphasis on American politics and policy issues and youth training in the United States. Although this book does not analyze issues of organizational structure, a brief overview of Hadassah structure is warranted to better understand the group's approach to such issues as gender roles, identity, and politics. Hadassah members constituted the base of Hadassah. The membership ranged between 300,000 and 350,000 in the 1950s and 1960s. After membership, the Hadassah chapter served as the next link in the Hadassah chain. The national constitution allowed for one chapter per city bearing the name of the city. Chapters with membership over 750 could be broken down into sections of the city, and these groups bore the names of significant Jewish or Zionist activists. Each chapter and affiliated group retained separate officers, chair people, programming, and meeting locations. Groups and chapters fit into regional classifications with twenty-eight regions in the United States. Chapters paid dues to their respective regional headquarters. In addition, regions held regular conferences and board meetings, with chapter presidents serving as board members under the umbrella of a larger regional president and vice president. Local and regional presidents and officers were elected by the local chapter, group, or region. Each chapter had a constitution that fit the national model and elected a president, vice president, secretary, and treasurer. In addition, various chairwomen and officers that specialized in certain areas were appointed.[41]

The national board served as the central administrative organ of Hadassah for the entire community, composed of regional presidents and presidents of chapters with a membership of over 5,000. The national president was also elected at the national convention, and members elected at the national convention were also members of the national board. At the national convention, Hadassah members made decisions on policy matters and sealed these decisions in a series of resolutions. Delegates decided on policy matters through a voting process — chapters received slots for delegates according to size — 1 attendee per 150 members. In addition, the national board attended the national convention as did the vice presidents of regions over 5,000. An executive committee also existed, which had the authority to make decisions for the group in lieu of the convention. This was composed of national Hadassah officers and ten additional elected officials.[42]

In 2012, we often take for granted that the U.S. government views Israel as America's special ally, and a majority of Jews see their relationship to Israel as central to their sense of Jewishness. The women of Hadassah contributed to both American policy toward Israel and Jews' warm perceptions about Israel. Hadassah led over 300,000 Jewish women in Zionist and political directions.[43] Hadassah offered Hadassah members both a Zionist ideology and a sense of empowerment as Jewish women.

A STATE IS BORN: HADASSAH ADJUSTS TO THE NEW STATE OF ISRAEL AND THE POLITICAL COMPLEXITIES OF HOMELAND

On November 29th, 1947, a milestone was reached in the history of the world. In endorsing the plan to set up separate Jewish and Arab States in Palestine, the United Nations has ended 2,000 years of national homelessness for the Jewish people. The deep emotion experienced by the Jews throughout the world cannot be conveyed in words, for all the hopes and aspirations of Jewry, growing out of centuries of persecution and humiliation, tried to express themselves on this day of fulfillment.
— Reported in The Senior, *a Hadassah periodical*[1]

Politics—understood as both formal political activities and as the creation of identity and ideological positioning—played an important role in Hadassah. Indeed, the creation of a Jewish state after thousands of years brought about substantial ideological questions not only for all Jews but also particularly for those engaged in Zionist work. Among Hadassah goals were supporting the political legitimacy of a state for the Jewish people and developing social welfare programs to assist in this project. Both Hadassah's lobbying activity and philanthropic work served explicitly political purposes and carried political repercussions. This chapter outlines the beginnings of a political consciousness focused on the state of Israel and on the concomitant construction of an American Jewish women's identity based on political and social action. Although often dismissed in both the historical literature and by its male contemporaries as "just" a charity or a women's social club, Hadassah proved to be a central actor in the shaping of both health and education policy in Israel and domestic and foreign policy agendas in America.[2]

The types of philanthropic work that Hadassah focused on reflected political agendas and had political consequences. As the largest Zionist membership organization for the greater part of the twentieth century, Hadassah served as a site from which to construct new forms of Jewish identity. As Jerold Auerbach has argued once, "Jewish statehood explicitly threatened the comfortable terms of American acculturation, Zionism was recast as Americanism, and Israel, in turn, became a miniature replica of the United States."[3] Auerbach credits Szold, Judah Magnes, and progressive lawyer Louis Brandeis for the American Jewish ideological merging of Zionism and Americanism with liberal American values.[4] Although Szold died in 1948, her liberal Americanized worldview persisted in the organization and crystallized in the postwar era.

One dimension that presented complexities for this combining of patriotism, liberalism, and Zionism in Hadassah rhetoric was the complicated issue of the Israeli and Jewish relationship with the Arabs. In the years immediately before and after the establishment of the State of Israel, Hadassah struggled with many ideological questions. Hadassah's effort to define Arab-Jewish relations became a significant area of contestation. In its early period, the leaders of Hadassah had adopted a culturally pluralistic and at times radical approach to Arab-Jewish relations that promoted a vision of Arab-Jewish coexistence.[5] Over the years, however, a more complicated discourse on Arabs surfaced that came to a head with the establishment of the state of Israel and the subsequent War of Independence.

THE EARLY DAYS

From its inception, Hadassah dealt with discrimination from its male-dominated peer organizations. Historian Mary McCune argues that Hadassah, in its formative period, struggled to be accepted by a male-dominated Jewish society engaged in a crusade to "overturn contemporary stereotypical presentations of Jewish men as weak."[6] As the Zionist movement increasingly equated the salvation of the Jewish people and the establishment of a state with the "New Jewish Man," the women of Hadassah, McCune argues, "exhibited a strong sense of gender consciousness, and they were, at the very least, well aware of women's subordinate position within the larger American Zionist movement."[7]

Hadassah in its early period presented a progressive and sometimes radical approach to the world, emphasizing cultural inclusiveness, class and gender consciousness, and harmony between Arabs and Jews. By the early state period, however, new and conflicting messages about identity, class, gender, and race came into conflict with earlier Hadassah ideological hallmarks.[8]

The roles of Jewish immigrant women in America were different from those they had generally played in their countries of origin. America allowed for increased women's participation in public organizations. As Paula Hyman has argued, during the transition from working-class immigrants to middle-class "Americans," Jewish immigrant women in America increasingly took on the responsibilities of transmitting Jewish culture to the next generations — in contrast to the generations of their parents and grandparents, which had placed the father as primary authority in the transmission of Jewish education. The adoption of a bourgeois domestic sphere ideology placed women in the role of both homemaker and Jewish educator. Women now bore the responsibility for sustaining Jewish identity within the home. Hyman explains:

> Bourgeois culture thus expected women to be at least moderately religious, certainly more religious than men, since they were deemed inherently more spiritual. The bourgeois division of labor between the sexes also conferred responsibility upon women for religiously based "good works," including the basic religious education of children.[9]

During the Progressive era, Jewish women, like their Christian counterparts, extended this domestic privilege to the public sphere by forming Jewish philanthropic organizations.[10]

Henrietta Szold, founder and revered matriarch of Hadassah, understood that for Jewish women, Zionism provided a means to engage in a variety of issues. Zionism served as a bridge between Judaism or Jewishness and politics. In a letter she wrote on the subject of Zionism and Judaism, she stated:

> We in New York haven't a conception of Jewish laxity — the distance between the Jews and Judaism. It is not a question of reform and orthodoxy — it is Judaism and non-Judaism. Zionism is the only anchor in sight. Here is the problem in its nakedness. How is it to be solved? I say through Zionism. [11]

Hadassah offered Jewish women a way to be Jewish that drew on different strengths and interests than traditional forms of Jewish participation.

World War II, the Holocaust, and the simultaneous legitimization of Zionist causes provided Jewish women a new platform of public expression that stressed political action in addition to philanthropic work. Organizations such as Hadassah could be counted among the most influential Jewish organizations of the 1940s and 1950s.[12]

Although acceptance of Zionism stands today as a central ideological tenant of many American Jews, Zionism has not always had the blanket acceptance of the American Jewish community. In fact, in the early twentieth century, the majority of Jews would not have identified themselves as Zionists, and many would have challenged the concept completely, finding it threatening to their newfound identity as Americans. While Zionist participation increased during the early part of the twentieth century, most historians agree that the Holocaust greatly increased American Jewish acceptance of Zionism. Aaron Berman has shown that during the Depression, Zionist groups found themselves in a crisis, as the economic problems in the United States seemed to draw the attention of the Jews. However, the Holocaust era brought Jews together. In particular, Zionist organizations and leaders once peripheral to the American Jewish community took center stage.[13] Israel gained popularity in a Jewish American community shocked and traumatized by the murder of six million Jews. Increasingly, Zionist influence on the American Jewish community became almost "hegemonic."[14]

HADASSAH AND THE HOLOCAUST

Many historians have criticized the American Jewish community for not doing enough to save European Jews from the Nazis. In particular, many argue that the Jews of America did not fight hard enough for the admission of more Jews into the United States. Other scholars maintain that American Jews feared that their allegiance to the United States would be questioned if they pushed to change the restrictive quotas.[15] On the other hand, Melvin Urofsky contends that leaders like

Brandeis and Felix Franfurter did attempt to negotiate with Roosevelt over the immigration quota, but to no avail.[16] Whatever the case may be, it is clear that when met with the crisis of the Holocaust American Jews emphasized the establishment of a Jewish homeland in Palestine as the antidote to anti-Semitic oppression.[17]

Although most Zionist organizations focused on the establishment of the State of Israel, Hadassah engaged in direct action successfully rescuing more than 50,000 Jewish children and teenagers from Germany and Eastern Europe between 1934 and1948 through a program called Youth Aliyah. Scholar Aaron Berman argues that Hadassah was the most successful American Jewish organization "at latching onto and exploiting concern for Germany."[18] Youth Aliyah had been designed to supply Palestine with eager new *halutzim,* immigrants who would work the land and contribute to the Jewish community.[19] However, as events unfolded in Europe, the program shifted to a rescue project. While some scholars, such as Sandra Berliant Kadosh, criticize Youth Aliyah for not going far enough in its efforts, one cannot deny that this program remains an example of one of the most successful efforts to save the Jews of Europe.

In a pamphlet published during World War II, "Why I belong to Hadassah," the impact of the Holocaust was addressed, and a new discourse on Zionism and Americanism came to the forefront:

> I belong to Hadassah because I want to see Justice done to my people as to all peoples of the earth. The concentration camps, the murder trains, the mass graves all over Europe-the thought often penetrates everything I think of. Everyday that I enjoy the inalienable right to life, liberty and the pursuit of happiness, millions of men, women and children are tortured and slain because they are Jews, like me.[20]

The quintessential document of American freedom, the Declaration of Independence, acted as a mirror for Jewish independence in a Jewish homeland where the "right to life, liberty and the pursuit of happiness" would be granted. The pamphlet goes on for several pages, arguing that "the dignity and worth of the Jews will be recognized and respected only if Jewish People, like all peoples, have a homeland."[21]

HADASSAH LOBBIES FOR THE NEW STATE

The "Jewish State Is Born!" exclaimed the *Hadassah Headlines* in their December 1947 issue. Responding to the historic passage of the UN Partition Plan, Hadassah leaders hurried to circulate the news via telegram to all chapter presidents:

> In this hour of triumph for justice and right we join the Jews of Palestine in their jubilation and vibrate to the joy of Europe's many thousands who are ready to pour from the dismissal camps to the welcoming gates of the Jewish state.[22]

As Hadassah and other Zionist organizations had hoped and worked for, a new Jewish land would finally be the haven of the Jews of Europe. However, the Hadassah leadership recognized that the drive for the political and economic success of the state had to continue and that in many ways the battle had just begun.[23]

Hadassah members and leadership had actively lobbied the U.S. government to support partition. As former Miami Beach Region President Jean Jacobson recalled:

> From the National office of Hadassah poured form letters suggesting formats for contacting President Truman, the Secretary of State, and the American UN representative. Chapter committees created dozens of suggested telegrams and flooded Lake Success (the site of the meetings) with them; anyone else in a position of influence we could possibly think of, we flooded with composed and intelligent arguments to support the Zionist position.[24]

In November 1947, Hadassah held its thirty-third annual convention. Rather than a social gathering, the event had a substantial political component. As often was the case, several prominent political leaders gave speeches and held roundtables during the five day convention. The speakers included leaders such as the Zionist activist and future president of Israel, Chaim Weizmann; chairman of the American branch of the Jewish Agency executive and prominent Zionist figure, Abba Hillel Silver; a representative from the United Nations and Mrs. Rose Halprin, the newly elected president of Hadassah, the only woman on the American branch of the Jewish Agency Executive Committee.[25]

Various issues were stressed at this meeting, including medical advancements needed to ensure the health and security of the emergent state. With a great sense of urgency, the necessity of land acquisition in Palestine took top priority at the convention. Judge Morris Rothenberg, president of the Jewish National Fund, argued that, "if a state is created, the land will still belong to Jews and Arabs who are citizens of Palestine; and every inch needed for expansion of Jewish Settlement will have to be bought and paid for from the rightful owners."[26] The philanthropic work done by Hadassah was thus political in nature. Land development in particular remained a central cause of Hadassah in the prestate and early state period. Land purchase was a political process, although it entailed fund raising, because it paved the way for Jews to claim ownership of land in Israel.[27]

Hadassah spent its budget on not just charitable endeavors that also carried political significance. The way in which monies were collected and delegated displayed the political nature of Hadassah fund-raising efforts. The budget approved for 1947 was $4,720,000. Of that money, $1,750,000 went to the Hadassah medical organization in Palestine, which served as the medical backbone of operations to Jewish fighters in battles over Jerusalem and during the independence war. Youth Aliyah, the program that transplanted youth from abroad to Palestine, received $1,700,000. Another $650,000 was directed to the Jewish National Fund for its "land purchase and restoration fund." An allocation of $120,000 provided funds for "Zionist Youth activities" in the United States and $500,000 to child welfare and vocational education.[28] Much of this philanthropic aid served political as well as humanitarian goals. In addition, the money was not simply distributed to other organizations. All of these programs, with the exception of land purchase, were Hadassah initiatives and run by Hadassah with help from the Yishuv.

Hadassah leaders realized that in addition to all of the efforts listed above, political pressure and education of the American public — both Jewish and non-Jewish — would play a central role in the outcome of the tensions over Israel. By putting pressure on the American government and the United Nations, Hadassah hoped to guarantee support for the Jews of Palestine. "We are entitled to claim from the United Nations financial and military assistance to enable us to stand on our feet properly."[29]

As part of the effort to educate and lobby, Hadassah's leadership produced political "kits" for "letters and speeches" to be used to "arm speakers" in the war of public relations.

> We cannot repeat too often the need to create a climate of public opinion favorable to the Israeli cause. Every political chairman who has taken it upon herself to disseminate the facts behind the distortions... does a service not only to Israel but to Democracy.[30]

The "political line" emphasized by the leadership stressed the failure of the world to enforce the UN partition plan and stem Arab assaults on Jewish targets and the apparent collusion of the British.

> "With the passive, and some say even overt aid of the British government in Palestine, the Arab league is getting bolder in its attempts to blackmail the UN. *This is an attempt by violence to render impotent the first great decision of the UN.*"[31] (Italics are original to the document.)

Jean Jacobson, former Miami Beach Region president, remembers that she received a Hadassah promotions packet with "suggested public service radio scripts for possible use in our local communities."[32] Through contacts at a local CBS radio station, Jacobson secured six thirty-minute timeslots where she spoke about Hadassah and Zionism. The shows were such a success that she parlayed them into a weekly radio variety show.[33]

U.S. policy and inaction, some kit materials argued, "has not been blameless either." The failure of the United States to support an initiative to bring an "International Police force to the Area" coupled with the U.S. ban on the "shipment of firearms to the Middle East" proved a source for great criticism. Hadassah encouraged its members to critique current policies and failure and to lobby for U.S. aid to the Yishuv.[34] Hadassah speakers were encouraged to "seize every opportunity that presents itself" to spread the word. Outside groups like "church groups, the League of Women Voters, the American Association of University Women, are just a few of the channels." Even speaking engagements in "hotel resorts" are described in Hadassah political kits as offering "an opportunity to show Arab aggression up in a proper light."[35]

As an organization, Hadassah's membership experienced tremendous growth in the period of the Independence War. By 1948, it totaled 250,000, which included 977 chapters and groups within the United States, extending throughout every state in the union.[36] During the early conflict over Palestine and the War of Independence in 1948, Hadassah provided medical aid and support to the Haganah, the precursor to the IDF (Israeli Defense Forces). While many in the first wave of Hadassah leaders immigrated to Palestine in the 1920s, by 1947, most Hadassah members had never set foot in Palestine.[37] They were, however, keenly aware of the support given to the effort in Palestine and the political nature of this aid.[38] As Mrs. David B. Greenberg, chair of Hadassah's thirty-fourth national gathering, and Mrs. David Stein of Philadelphia, who was co-chair, stated in a press release:[39]

> In the crucial battle around Jerusalem, where the bitterest fighting took place, every Jewish soldier who went into the field was armed with the knowledge that Hadassah doctors and nurses were standing by, ready to help and heal. The Hadassah hospital at Mt. Scopus did not surrender — neither British pressure nor Arab Ambushes and shell fire prevented its gallant staff from carrying on its job... Shells are still falling around the Hadassah hospital in the holy city.[40]

At the annual conference held in November 1948 in Atlantic City, 5,000 delegates and guests met to discuss the future of the state of Israel and the ways in which Hadassah could be an active participant in its building.[41] Several resolutions were adopted at the convention that reflected the political nature of the organization. Support of the State of Israel remained a central theme in the resolutions adopted. "Hadassah, the Women's Zionist Organization of America, in convention assembled for their first time since the establishment of the State of Israel... Pledges its continued support to the end that Israel shall be a nation of peace and security among the nations of the world."[42] In addition, Hadassah pronounced its approval of David Ben Gurion as the "first Prime Minister of the provisional government of Israel."[43]

In its self-proclaimed "political" resolution, Hadassah urged the United States to support the establishment of Israel. The "responsibility" of the United States to broker a peaceful resolution to the conflict was stressed. "Flagrant acts of aggression" on the part of

Arabs were described as "a threat to world peace."[44] Appealing to the U.S. government not only on behalf of Hadassah members but also on behalf of "American citizens and men of goodwill everywhere," the resolution chastised the United Nations because it "has taken no action demanding the withdrawal from Israel of the invading armies of six Arab states."[45]

Hadassah continued to support the relocation of young American adults and youth to Israel, or *haluziut,* as a viable option without facing accusations of dual allegiance. The first wave of Hadassah leaders subscribed heavily to the notion that the best way to aid the Jews of Palestine was to actually move to the Yishuv. Unlike many of the male-dominated Zionist organizations, Hadassah firmly encouraged this movement to Israel as a means of political and personal fulfillment. Most of the *halutzim* (men and women pioneers) had been either Eastern European or Sephardic Jews already living in parts of the Middle East. After the formation of Hadassah, middle-class American Jewish women like Alice Seligsberg and Henrietta Szold moved to Palestine.[46] As Szold explained, "not all the haluzot (female pioneers) come from Eastern Europe. Some come from America, and they are haluzot even if they can dance... and do all sorts of society stunts."[47] Here Szold tried to break the gender and class stereotypes, which suggested that female pioneers lacked culture and social etiquette. Szold argued that sophisticated American women could participate in the pioneer movement without having to compromise their social standing.

As time went on, the organization continued to sponsor movement to Israel, but aliyah became a less central aspect of Hadassah work because of an expansion of membership into a more mainstream population. With the establishment of the State of Israel, Hadassah "intensified" its program of halutziut and shifted the focus away from the leadership and to the youth:

> Hadassah understands the importance of an alert, intelligent and informed Zionist youth. We endorse the principle of halutziut, which trains young American Jews who wish to make their future in the Jewish State. We know that our youth has technical skills, moral courage, physical strength and high idealism, qualities which should be of inestimable service to the Jewish State.[48]

This encouragement of youth to move to Palestine did not, according to a Hadassah article, "represent a new departure. Throughout its history Hadassah had a program of practical work in Palestine... We are geared to intensify our activities until such a time as the Zionist objective is fully realized."[49]

Idealized in the 1920s for communing and working the land in the Jewish people's ancestral home, halutziut was respected by Szold and her contemporary Lotta Levansohn.[50] The image of the halutz popularized through film, poetry, folk songs, and other cultural texts captured the imagination of youth involved in Hadassah in the coed youth program Young Judea, which Hadassah sponsored beginning in the 1930s. During the War for Independence, halutzim volunteered in droves and assisted in the defense of the new nation. In the poststate era between 1946 and 1952, halutziut reached its zenith of popularity, and former participants of Young Judea and of the Hadassah program for young women Junior Hadassah volunteered for service.[51]

In 1949, at its thirty-fifth annual convention held in San Francisco, Hadassah adopted a resolution that described Hadassah's support of halutziut. The wording of this resolution relied heavily on the language of Americanism and contained much defensive language that preempted any accusations of double allegiance. The resolution stated that some Americans Jews "will be moved to pioneer in the tradition of America," and these youngsters will "provide American know-how" to the "world's youngest democracy."[52] Patriotic language remained a constant avenue from which to counter criticism and to assert an allegiance to both Israel and America.

The pioneer, idealized in the Jewish community as a hero of conscience and strength, often was juxtaposed with a less-than-glorified picture of an incompetent Arab seeking the help of Jewish know-how.[53]

NOTIONS ABOUT ARABS

As a result of the UN resolution and the ensuing battles and eventual establishment of the State of Israel, Hadassah attitudes toward Arabs gradually shifted. Hadassah in many ways became a more conservative organization regarding this issue. One area in which this was apparent was in the representations and analysis of Arabs and Arab states within the ranks of Hadassah. Hadassah's portrayals and coverage of Arab-Jewish relations provide further evidence of the highly political nature of the organization. Hadassah was political in the traditional sense of lobbying, as well as by supporting activities in Palestine. It was also political in creating and defining images of Arabs and the Arab world for a generation of Jewish women and their friends and families.

In both actions and words, the leadership and rank and file of Hadassah negotiated between a new hard-line approach to Arabs and the original pluralistic and inclusive paradigm that its founders had articulated. To fully understand the change in Hadassah attitudes, It is important to first look to a period when Arab-Jewish relations were not so fixed in a binary opposition as they are today but rather were characterized by a fluid set of ideological and historical factors.

Henrietta Szold, the founder and revered matriarch of Hadassah, believed that Arabs and Jews could live side by side in a binational state. A progressive at heart, Szold ideologically aligned herself with the school of cultural pluralism and had great affinity for historical abolitionists who had fought against slavery in the United States before the Civil War. She strongly believed in securing expanded rights for minority and immigrant groups in America.[54] As historian Marc Brown argues, Szold transferred these world views to Arab-Jewish relations when she moved to Palestine. Alongside American Jewish leaders like Martin Buber and Judah Magnes, Szold served on the executive committee of Ihud, a political organization founded with the goal of establishing a binational state in Palestine. Szold drew a parallel between black-white issues in the United States and Arab-Jewish problems. She saw the animosity between Jews and Arabs in racial terms and worried that Jews would develop racist attitudes toward Arabs and vice versa.[55]

Hadassah leaders pushed beyond the boundaries of Progressivism.[56] Hadassah leaders provided a critical approach to class dynamics that would have been "several shades too 'red' for America in general," argues Naomi Lichtenberg.[57] Thus, Hadassah leaders pushed the boundaries of a Progressive ideology, incorporating aspects of the cultural pluralism and social welfare attitudes of the movement, and adding a Socialist class-oriented analysis and a desire to break the mold of genteel society.

This also allowed for a more radical approach toward Arabs. Elements of early Hadassah ideology, in particular the emphasis on racial equality and cultural pluralism, formed in this period would resonate with Hadassah members throughout the post–World War II era.

As Naomi Lichtenberg eloquently argues, Henrietta Szold and her contemporaries wanted to live in peace with their Arab "cousins" and welcomed "diversity in Palestine that did not exclude Arabs."[58] Hadassah leadership viewed racism toward Arabs as a disease:

> Our history and the history of our Arab cousins show that we have too many spiritual and intellectual points of contact with each other... On this we build our hopes — on this and on the determination to remove from our national aspirations every possible admixture of injustice. If our course is just, wholly just, and righteous, we are bound to find just and righteous and peaceful means of conciliation. We shall ally ourselves with the best of our Arab fellows, to cure what is diseased in us and in them.[59]

This approach to Arab-Jewish relations was shared by most of the Hadassah leadership during the 1920s and into the 1930s.

Over time, as hostilities became more apparent and as the struggle for land came to a boiling point in the early state period, Hadassah negotiated between the adoption of a more hawkish approach to Arab-Jewish relations and the incorporation of the early values of acceptance and harmony. When the UN partition plan failed to be recognized by Palestinian Arabs and other Arab States alike, the rhetoric of Hadassah necessarily became more complex. On the one hand, Hadassah portrayed Arabs as the enemy; on the other hand, compassion for Arabs by Jews was consistently stressed. Here we see a new, more hawkish approach to Arabs as a result of political realities, existing alongside a commitment to a cultural pluralist viewpoint.

Although a binational plan may seem unimaginable to many in the early twenty-first century, at the time of the passage of the UN Partition Plan in 1947, many American Jews felt that Arabs would welcome the opportunity to live with Jews. *The Hadassah Newsletter* coverage of the event claimed, "A growing number of Arabs in Palestine want to live in peace with their Jewish neighbors. They see in the decision a definitive solution, which, if accepted by both parties, can end the political turmoil of the last decade."[60]

As hostilities increased, depictions of the Arab threat grew more vivid and frightening. Several Hadassah magazines ran an ad that was used by Hadassah to raise funds and membership. The advertisement shows a "Jewish doctor shot in the back" with his blood spilling on the ground. Based on actual events, the ad explains how Dr. Hugo Lehrs of Hadassah, "a man who refused to desert his Arab patients," was shot after "two Arab colleagues walking with him stepped aside when the murderer asked 'which is the Jew.'"[61] Here we see the betrayal of a Jewish man who faithfully extended his services to Arabs free of charge. This theme of betrayal would become increasingly dominant in Hadassah publications.

By viewing Arab hostilities as a betrayal of Jewish kindness, Hadassah leaders struggled to maintain a balance between its newfound hawkishness and its historical cultural pluralism. By describing the violence as a betrayal, Hadassah maintained its image as a healer of all peoples in the face of the violence. The ad goes on to describe the murder of Nurse Hanna Gardi, "a refugee from a concentration camp, a girl who had come to Palestine to succor the sick no matter what their race or creed."[62] Hadassah's pluralism is juxtaposed with the viciousness of Arab brutality and betrayal. The *Hadassah Newsletter* ran this ad along with two cover stories that read "Arabs Attack Hospital" and "Arabs Still Come for Treatment."[63] Again, the violence of Arabs provides a context from which to view Hadassah's commitment of treating of Arab patients as extremely open minded in the face of Arab hostilities. [64]

Even worse than the Arabs, the British are depicted as the two-faced force providing Arabs with the necessary tools for victory and as using "neutrality" as a shield to assist the Arab assault. The cartoon showed a menacing Arab figure in traditional garb holding a gun and a sword; it reads, "British 'neutrality' pulls the strings."[65] In April 1948, the worst possible scenario was reported at the Western Wall: "Judaism's holiest shrine has been occupied by Arab invaders without the opposition of the so-called security forces of the British. Above a young Iraqi, armed with a machine gun, a soldier stands guard while in the background a Palestinian policeman looks on unconcernedly."[66]

As conditions worsened on the ground, Hadassah's language became more militaristic in tone. Captions like "Mobilize for the Jewish State" underscored the sense of urgency and responsibility that Hadassah felt with regard to its fledgling state.[67] For the first time in Hadassah literature, Arabs were described as being engaged in a "Holy War." Such language is common today, but it was only beginning to come into use at that point.[68] Even a set of Jewish New Year greeting cards put out by Hadassah reflected the new militarism. The cards, designed as a fund-raising series, included a box of twelve Rosh Hashanah cards at the price of $1 per box. The cards featured Israeli art — with one card showing an Israeli fighter holding a military rifle, with a caption underneath reading Happy New Year in Hebrew.[69] Indeed, the Israeli pioneer that had been represented in the past primarily as an agricultural worker increasingly was associated with "defense."[70]

At the same time, while hostilities and bloodshed escalated, Hadassah members continued to point to the group's open and accepting policies toward Arabs. In keeping with its roots of inclusion and equal opportunity, Hadassah allowed Arabs access to Hadassah resources in Palestine. While becoming more hawkish in its political assessment of Arabs and Arab states, Hadassah maintained this inclusive approach and argued that the new State of Israel ameliorated the situation of Arabs. Among the many advantages to Arabs in Israel, Hadassah reported that Arab children "benefit" from a higher standard of education in Israel's state-sponsored Arab public schools. Children learned Hebrew and English as second languages in a free public school system. Israel, readers are assured, would not abandon its Arab brethren.[71] By extension, Hadassah's support and involvement in Israel were perceived as compatible with American progressive principles.

Arab farmers also benefited from Israel's programs and loans. Israel, *Hadassah Headlines* reported, wanted to uplift the Arab population: "As long as this large minority remains economically and socially retarded, the entire nation's well being is prejudiced."[72]

Baltimore radio talk show host Ian Macfarlane and his wife reported to Hadassah after a trip to Europe, visiting the Displaced Person camps of Holocaust survivors and the extermination camps at Austerlitz and Chelmno. They concluded the trip by visiting Israel and Hadassah Medical Center. In contrast to the sites of genocide they had witnessed in Europe, of Hadassah Medical Center they wrote, "There is no discrimination of any kind in this house of healing."[73] They were impressed that Arabs, Christians, Muslims, and Jews were equally treated well at the hospital. The Wynnewood, Pennsylvania, chapter reminded its members that Hadassah medical facilities cared "for all — Jews and Arabs alike."[74]

Every month, *Hadassah Newsletter* ran a column entitled "Diary of a Jerusalem Housewife." It provided full detailed, diary-like coverage of Jerusalem under siege. This column became one of the most popular *Hadassah Newsletter* columns in the 1940s and 1950s. As Esther Kesselman, Hadassah National Board Member from 1947 to 1950, recalled, "Hers was always the first column I read when the newspaper arrived. She would write about the handsome young Zionist she married, their three children, and how hard life as a pioneer could be. We shared her joys and tribulations. She was our family and we loved her."[75] Since most Hadassah rank and file members never went to Palestine, unlike in the early days, columns such as these brought the halutz experience home to America. Molly wrote candidly and vividly about day-to-day life in Palestine, bringing a personal eyewitness account of many aspects of life, including Arab-Jewish relations. Describing a recent siege in Jerusalem, Molly explained how she cried alone when no one was looking, and she thought, "how we went out in the shelling day after day to get our bucket of water and 140 grammes of bread... how concerts were held for the boys as the bombs fell about."[76] Molly's personal accounts detailed the difficulties and joys of life in Jerusalem. Much of her coverage dealt with her perceptions and anger toward Arabs. These emotions were transmitted to Hadassah readers. Molly became such a popular Hadassah fixture that she packed audiences on Hadassah speaking tours in the United States.[77]

Hadassah leadership and its publications endorsed a complex approach toward Arabs. The cultural pluralism adopted by Hadassah's founders remained a central tenant of Hadassah ideology, and Arabs always received access to social and medical programs in Israel. Hadassah members learned of the benefits Arabs received under the Israeli government. These conclusions, of course, contradict many Palestinian accounts of the impact of the War of Independence on their lives, for this is a history that is highly contested. Whatever historical narrative one accepts, it is clear that Arabs in Israel and Arab refugees encountered both positive and negative repercussions after the war and that the picture painted by Hadassah beginning in 1947 neglects the possible dark aspects of that portion of Israeli history.[78]

While Hadassah made great efforts to ensure that an open-door policy existed toward the Arab population, tensions in the Middle East shifted the ways in which Hadassah portrayed Arabs. The discourse on Palestinians and Arab states became more complex as the decades progressed, and a hybrid picture of good, bad, and indifferent Arab characters surfaced in Hadassah literature.

In the period before and immediately after the establishment of the State of Israel, Hadassah engaged in political activities and shaped the way in which many Jewish women and their families viewed their identity as Jews and Americans. Rather than distancing itself from activities in Israel once statehood was granted, Hadassah strengthened its political and humanitarian efforts for Israel.

While they worked to help others, the women of Hadassah also struggled to understand their roles as women and as Jewish Americans. At the same time that Hadassah worked to politicize Jewish women, it also retained certain traditional gender norms. As the 1950s, the era of June Cleaver and McCarthy, approached, notions about gender and identity became more complicated. During the 1950s in America, not just Jewish women but many women in America struggled to understand their true place in society and within the family structure. At the same time, American liberalism itself came under fire as anti-Communist hysteria led many to distance themselves from any activity that could be misconstrued as "Communist." For Hadassah "ladies" these issues would play themselves out in complicated and often conflicting ways.

CHAPTER II

A 'BULWARK AGAINST COMMUNISM': HADASSAH'S POLITICAL ACTIVISM IN FOREIGN POLICY DURING THE 1950S

As World War II ended, a new war based on suspicion, fear, and international dominance — the Cold War — emerged. In this climate, the new state of Israel emerged as a pawn in the game of geopolitics. As the Cold War descended upon the Middle East, Hadassah sought to secure Israel's position as an American ally by showing how Israel's goals aligned with American interests. On the domestic scene, however, Hadassah worked to oppose McCarthyite witch hunts, and it supported an expansion of civil rights. Playing both sides of the Cold War coin, Hadassah utilized anti-Communist rhetoric in order to ensure American political and economic support for Israel while at the same time fighting for the liberal democratic ideals that had been part and parcel of Hadassah's philosophy since its progressive inception.

After the establishment of the State of Israel in 1948, Hadassah shifted its emphasis to supporting state building and continued fund-raising for programs already in place. It also sought to ensure that leaders within the U.S. government and the business sector as well as the American, and specifically the Jewish public, continued to support the nascent state both politically and financially. Hadassah leadership lobbied various groups to support Israel and to ensure that Israel emerged as a close ally of the United States. This alliance between Israel and the United States resulted from pressure by groups like Hadassah that both worked to cement the political ties between the two countries and to instill in Jewish people a sense of obligation and pride in support of Israel. The aftermath of World War II and the Holocaust greatly increased the popularity of Zionism within the Jewish community in America. However, the challenge of merging an American Jewish identity with support of Israel often brought fear of accusations of dual allegiance. By focusing on Americanism during World War II, Hadassah drew connections between Israel and the United States.

Figure 1. "Join Hadassah" Hangtag from 1957. The back of the tag reads, "It's good Americanism to Join Hadassah."

Photo Courtesy of Hadassah, The Women's Zionist Organization of America.

HADASSAH OPERATIONS

Hadassah's membership in the United States invested monies and manpower in various Israeli projects. Hadassah Hebrew University Medical Center in Jerusalem, Hadassah's primary investment, housed several medical institutions. These institutions included the hospital, the Kiryat Hayovel family and community center, and the Nathan and Lina Strauss Health Center. Hadassah also sponsored vocational projects in Israel, such as the Brandeis Vocational Training Center, the Hadassah Vocational Guidance Institute and Hadassah Neurim Vocational Training Center of Youth Aliyah, and the Henrietta Szold School of Nursing. Hadassah also served as the largest single contributor to the Jewish National Fund (JNF), an organization that was responsible for purchasing land for Jewish development. From its founding to 1968, Hadassah donated, through JNF, 83 million trees and "reclaimed" 625,000 dunams of land.[1]

Hadassah also operated several vocational training schools in Israel. Some were housed at the Brandeis Center in Jerusalem — such as the Alice l. Seligsberg vocational high school, which taught students to become dressmakers, fashion designers, cooks, secretaries, and provided "domestic citizenship and post-graduate vocational training." [2] The Brandeis Center in Romema housed Hadassah's Fine Mechanics and Instruments School and the Printing School.[3] In 1950, Hadassah opened a hotel school in cooperation with the Israeli government that offered a two-year course in hotel management. In addition, a variety of rural education programs were offered at the Hadassah-Neurim site.[4]

Hadassah maintained several programs focused on its work in the United States, including American Affairs, Zionist Affairs, leadership training seminars, study circles, educational programs, and more. Hadassah strongly supported the United Nations and in 1953 sent 5,000 women to the United Nations, more women than any other nongovernmental organization (NGO).[5] Hadassah also had several departments, including a publicity department. The New School for Social Research evaluated the Hadassah promotional materials department: "Probably no other non-profit organization in the country can match the effectiveness and scope of Hadassah's literature. The folders appeal to the eye and they go straight to the point with essential facts." In 1953 alone, 1,683,000 copies of 41 different pamphlets were distributed by the Hadassah promotions department.[6]

Several publications, including *Hadassah Newsletter* and later *Hadassah Magazine*, were sent to over 350,000 members. They constituted the "largest single subscription group of any Anglo-Jewish publication in the world."[7] *Hadassah Magazine*, which replaced *Hadassah Newsletter* in 1960, boasted a readership of over one million. In addition, Hadassah circulated to its members and potential members hundreds of thousands of pamphlets, brochures, and kits. Hadassah also produced histories, videos, and cookbooks. In 1956 alone,

Hadassah-affiliated researchers published 1,300 papers.[8] In the fiscal year of 1969, Hadassah's total budget (funds raised) amounted to a whopping $12,381,017; of that, over 50 percent went to the Hadassah Medical Organization, 18 percent to Youth Aliyah, 6 percent to the Jewish National Fund, 1 percent to youth activities, and 5 percent to Israel education.[9]

HADASSAH'S PRO-ISRAEL LOBBY

U.S. foreign policy interest in the Mediterranean area increased as a result of postwar tensions and U.S. intervention in Turkey and Greece. The Palestine question also captured the interest of foreign policy experts in the postwar era. The movement for the establishment of a new state for the Jews gained new ground in light of new evidence of Holocaust atrocities. Truman sided with the Jews in the debate, realizing that his political career might benefit from Jewish votes. In contrast, he explained, "I do not have hundreds of thousands of Arabs among my constituents."[10]

In the 1950s, Hadassah expanded on the rhetoric of Americanization employed during World War II by using foreign policy Cold War rhetoric that contended that Soviet aggression threatened to overrun entire geographical regions and that the United States needed to contain Communism by supporting regimes that supported democratic values in the face of this threat. The red menace, according to this theory, had reared its ugly head and was threatening to destroy Eastern Europe and Asia, and, as Hadassah stressed, the Middle East. Hadassah argued that Israel could "help defend the Middle East" against "Soviet objectives in the Middle East."[11]

Cold War tensions swept into the Middle East, further dividing Arab nations from Israel, and fueled the military aspirations of neighboring countries like Egypt. The United States would eventually champion Israel, while the USSR would support Syria and Egypt. Hadassah seized the moment to suggest that Israel held one solution to possible Soviet world domination, in order to argue for the necessity of U.S. financial and political support of Israel. In an article entitled "Sputnik and Other

Russian Gains Place New Demand for Positive US Program in the Middle East," Hadassah's Zionist Affairs chair, Mrs. Halprin, explained that "Russia's recent and spectacular gains in the scientific, political and propaganda fields have jolted American citizens into a new awareness of the seriousness of the global threat between Communism and the free world."[12] Halprin further explained that "Arab propagandists" often attempted to deflect the issue of the USSR's involvement by reframing friction as a "local" conflict. However, she argued, "this is a tactic to obscure the real issue, namely, that the ominous tension in the Middle East is only one manifestation of the conflict between democracy and communism, and a strategic battlefield in the cold war between Russia and the United States."[13]

American Cold War rhetoric painted the conflicts in the Middle East as a battle between the forces of Americanism and Communism. Israeli leadership and Hadassah alike portrayed Israel as a "bulwark" of democracy and anti-Communism in an increasingly Soviet-dominated map of the Middle East. And geopolitics drastically changed after Abdul Jamal Nasser rose to power in Egypt in the coup of 1952. A strident Arab nationalist with major political ambitions, Nasser purchased $320 million weapons from Czechoslovakia in 1955.[14] Syria also purchased weapons from the Eastern Bloc.[15] At the same time that Arab nations strengthened ties with the Soviets, Israelis feared that United States might enter into its own weapons deals with the Arab world in an effort to stem the tide.[16] Threatened by the accumulation of weaponry by Arab nations, Israel reached out to the American government for further arms assistance. After the Eisenhower administration failed to supply Israel with necessary weaponry, France became Israel's primary weapons supplier.[17]

Two months after Nasser decided to nationalize the Suez Canal and after the Egyptian arms deal with the USSR, Rose L. Halprin, former president of Hadassah and member of the Jewish Agency Executive, reported on a recent trip to Israel in the current events section of the *Hadassah Newsletter*:

> Since the Soviet Arms deal with Egypt a year ago, Israel and her friends have been exerting Herculean efforts to correct the imbalance of arms as a deterrent to Egyptian aggression... Israel could never afford to equal in quantity Egypt's bargain price goods from the Soviets. Israel seeks

a qualitative equality, based on a limited number of modern defense weapons in the hands of its devoted soldiers.[18]

In addition, she informed Hadassah members that retaliation to attacks from Egyptians served as a "defense measure."[19]

The cover of the November edition of *Hadassah Newsletter* read, "Israel Strike to End Arab Belligerence: Seek Permanent Peace." According to this article, "Menaced by the tightening noose of Soviet-armed Egyptian, Jordanian and Syrian troops under a joint command and goaded beyond endurance by the murderous forays of Egyptian *fedayeen* marauders, the Israel defense Army went into action. The announced objective was to destroy the bases of the fedayeen in the Sinai Peninsula and Gaza strip."[20] The article went on to defend Israel's actions in terms of a defensive act of reprisal, and it gave a detailed summary of the campaign. It also contained a piece entitled "Eyewitness Report from Israel." Written by Joan Comay, the article was constructed like a journal, with several dated entries. The author offered interested readers in America an "eyewitness" play-by-play account of what it felt like to be on the ground in Israel during such an undertaking. The format was similar to the monthly entries of the earlier "Diary of a Jerusalem Housewife," written as a first-person account of life in Israel meant to allow Hadassah members to feel connected to the struggle in Israel. "Jerusalem, the capital of Israel, woke up last Monday morning to a world without transport." Comay described how residents felt during wartime, she described how "older men were dressed in Khakis" as they began guard duty, and described how women participated by preparing the houses for blackouts. Comay conveyed the mood of angst and preparation of a people operating like a well-oiled machine, who were painfully accustomed to the wartime activities.[21]

Comay reported the triumph of Israel over its enemies with equally dramatic flair by harkening back to the biblical battle between Jews and Egyptians:

> We Israelis had fought a valiant fight against our ancient enemy, the Egyptians. Israelis had died once more for their right to be a free people, to cultivate their gardens in peace without fear of molestation. I looked up at the blue and white flag flying clear against the stars and I thought of

the ancient biblical story of Exodus and how G-d saved Israel as it crossed the Sinai desert on the way to the promised land. Dare one new hope that once more Israel will be firmly established in its land-its integrity guaranteed by international law and its safety secured by the courage of its people.[22]

While Hadassah members learned about the Suez Canal struggle in terms of geopolitics and the USSR, articles like this brought home the "defense strategy" that lay at the heart of Israel's involvement in Suez. In addition, by allowing Hadassah members to participate vicariously in the war through eyewitness reporting by a woman, Hadassah continued a literary technique employed in the Independence War. The eyewitness coverage by a woman of the Suez crisis impact on the Israeli community, on herself, and on her family brought to life the dangers faced by the Israelis and served to rally Hadassah women in the United States to the cause of defending Israel.

This perceived "triumph" proved to be short-lived. Although Israel, France, and the British made great strides toward capturing the canal in October and November of 1956, American political resistance, backed by the United Nations, halted their efforts. A dispute between Washington and Nasser had precipitated the nationalizing of the Suez Canal; the tripartite attack on Egypt had not included the United States, which had already voiced concern over military measures to quell the crisis. The USSR threatened to besiege Britain with atomic weapons if they did not retreat.[23] Eisenhower, furious over the "double-crossing" behavior of Israel, France, and Britain, applied diplomatic and economic pressure, going to the United Nations and withholding economic aid.[24] Israel removed its troops from the Suez Canal in March of 1957, and the United Nations then turned over the canal to the Egyptians.

Judith Epstein, Hadassah president from 1956 to 1960, reflected on her experience with the Suez crisis: "When I became president in November of 1956, we were suddenly shaken by the fact of the Sinai invasion." [25] With hindsight, she believed that if Britain had "moved faster" on the Suez crisis, the Suez and Sinai would be under European and Israeli control, and "the world situation today would have been entirely different in regard to the Middle East." While Hadassah played a role in the war through its medical efforts and political lobbying,

Epstein believes that "the major thrust of Hadassah at the time (although we had our political connections) as the powerful American Jewish women's organization played a real part in making the American public understand why Israel had gone to Sinai."[26] As a result of the Sinai invasion and the increased awareness of Israel's precarious position in the Middle East, Hadassah gained an additional 18,000 members.[27]

The Suez crisis somewhat damaged the relationship between Israel and the United States, but the continued image of Israel as a "bulwark against communism" served to remedy the discord. Hadassah continued to stress the importance of Israel for the balance of power in the Middle East, and their efforts appeared successful when the 1957 Eisenhower Doctrine solidified America's interventionist position with regard to the Middle East. The doctrine stated that the United States would offer aid to any country threatened by a Communist revolution. This did not signify a change in America's politics in the Middle East but rather further reinforced America's efforts to contain Communist and Soviet expansion in the region.[28]

On October 3, 1955, Hadassah dedicated its new national headquarters in New York. Mayor Wagner proclaimed the week of October 10 to 17 as Hadassah week in the metropolitan area. At the event, onlookers watched as national president Rebecca Shulman presented a $7 million check to the wife of the Israeli ambassador Abba Eban, reaching to a total fund-raising mark of $100 million raised since the organization's founding.[29] The featured speaker at the event was Jacob K. Javits, former Republican congressman and member of the House Foreign Affairs Committee. Javits, a longtime supporter of Israel, titled his talk "Israel: A Bulwark against Communism" and explained why the $250 million in grant monies given to Israel by the United States since 1950 served the purposes of both nation building in Israel but, most importantly, helped maintain the balance of power in the Middle East. The "Soviet arms race" in the Middle East could be thwarted by the maintenance of a democratic presence in Israel.[30]

In combination with stressing Israel's significance in establishing a pro-Western democracy in the Middle East, Hadassah leadership and its literature focused their attention on building solidarity among the Jewish people. Although the popularity of Zionism in the

United States among the Jewish community increased dramatically in response to World War II and the Holocaust, once the State of Israel was established, it was not a necessary conclusion that American Jews would see themselves as responsible for Israel's success. Therefore, in addition to lobbying political officials and influential people within the non-Jewish community, Hadassah worked hard to convince American Jews that their connection to Israel remained vital. A significant part of this approach emphasized the democratic values and principles of Israel. Israel was depicted as a democracy not too different from the United States.

Israel's importance, according to Hadassah, was not only as a haven for the world's Jews but also as the harbinger of democratic and American values in the Middle East. For Hadassah members, support for Israel went beyond Jewish identity and affiliation and extended into the vary safeguarding of Americanism in the world. At the Hadassah Midwinter Conference held in February 1955, Rose Halprin spoke of her recent trip to Israel and the amount of "soul-searching" that her fellow Hadassah regional presidents had experienced as a result of this trip. Halprin explained that Israel "is not alone," because Hadassah members stood with Israel to provide support. In Israel, Halprin said, "there is a deep feeling of aloneness and isolation. One feels humble in the presence of these people... in fact one even feels a little ashamed." At the same time, Halprin pleaded with the American Jewish community to heed the call of Israel for aid. "The American Jewish community does not yet understand the danger that threatens Israel."[31]

Hadassah publications, such as *Hadassah Newsletter* and *Hadassah Headlines,* encouraged members and their families to spread the word about the necessity of American political and economic support of Israel and the key role that American Jews were playing in ensuring the existence of Israel. Through their involvement in Hadassah, members received an education in foreign policy, American politics, and Jewishness. Hadassah indeed began to play a major role in constructing a new Cold War Jewish American women's identity that stressed the responsibility of American Jews to Israel in a Cold War context. In the 1950s, the notion that Israel should play a central role in the lives of American Jews, although gaining acceptance among the

Jewish community had not yet been solidified. Hadassah's work in educating and supplying Jewish women and their families with a new form of Jewish identity involved an emphasis on cultural and political affiliation.

Articles written by U.S. and Israeli political officials and experts, living in both nations, filled the pages of *Hadassah Newsletter* and *Hadassah Headlines*. While Hadassah members penned much of the material dealing with Jewish education, Hadassah functions, and membership drives, many of the articles dealing with foreign policy or domestic issues were educational and informative in nature, often written by men in positions of power. As might be expected, Hadassah leaders carefully selected what political positions to champion in their literature.[32]

AMERICANISM

Increasingly Hadassah harkened to a patriotic American language in order to shelter themselves from accusations of a dual state allegiance that made them insufficiently sensitive to the needs of the United States. In response to these anxieties, Hadassah merged notions of Zionism with a new found patriotic fervor, in a sense wrapping themselves in the American flag.[33] The language of Americanism began to take hold in Hadassah literature in the World War II era, and it remained dominant in Hadassah rhetoric through the 1950s and 1960s. During World War II, Hadassah, to legitimate the notion that democracy and American values like freedom and liberty should lead one to support Jewish Palestine and later Israel, Hadassah used Americanism and patriotism in its rhetoric. This began in World War II as a way of capitalizing on American patriotism. Messages like the following were published in Hadassah brochures:

> As an American Jew, surely you know that you cannot separate your fight to safeguard a democratic America from your fight to create a free world. In such a world there must and should be a place for a democratic Jewish Commonwealth in Palestine. It is all one fight, for the same principle-liberty and justice for all. Help us win it.[34]

The message of Jewish Americanism continued to remain useful as Jews sought to defend their allegiance to both the newborn state of Israel and to the United States. Later, this same language would be used to shield Hadassah against any McCarthyite charges of Communism.

Not just Jews but "American Citizens," the resolution stated, are "disillusioned" by the failure of the United States to secure support for Israel from the United Nations:

> THEREFORE BE IT RESOLVED that Hadassah.... Respectfully urge the President of the United States to instruct the United Nations to sponsor direct negotiations between Israel and the Arab States, with a view to securing a stable peace."[35]

This emphasis on "Americanism" in Hadassah rhetoric had originated in World War II, when patriotism to the nation dominated political and cultural discourse throughout the United States. Over time, this harkening to American values as justification for support of Israel and Zionism varied according to the historical circumstance. In the period of state development, the language of Americanism responded to the tremendous Jewish anxiety over the possible accusation that dual allegiance to America and Israel made Jews untrustworthy citizens of the United States. Rather than leaving American Zionists open to such criticism, Hadassah merged American values with Zionism. With the emergence of the Cold War, the use of American values and American language also served to place Zionist discourse squarely in the interest of democratic preservation.[36]

Other advertisements that were aimed at attracting new members and revitalizing existing members took a more gendered approach, one that was based on an appeal to motherhood. One read, "Because we are women of Hadassah we know nothing is ever born without pain." Along with this caption was a picture of a woman holding up a baby. The ad then invoked the language of Americanism: "Because we are Americans we of Hadassah know the new State of Israel, founded on democratic principles, must be assisted to become one of the family of nations. Only then can there be a true birth of freedom."[37]

Convention speeches, resolutions, newspaper coverage, and local meetings all relied heavily on American patriotism to ensure support of Israel and to defend against the possibility of accusation that Jews had a double allegiance to two countries.[38] A wall display published in the fall of 1948 by the publicity department of Hadassah, along with a brochure entitled "Because We Are Americans," served to outline the need for American support of Israel in patriotic language.[39] Israel would preserve key democratic principles for the free world. A "proud" American heritage served as the backdrop to support the goal of the "citizen builders" of Israel engaged in a struggle for "liberty and Justice for all." In order to secure Israel's position and "international peace and security," Hadassah would, among other actions, provide support in the areas of social welfare, health projects, and "land purchase."[40]

Hadassah's messages about Israel as a bulwark of democracy in the Middle East aligned Israel with the goals of the United States. Hadassah members addressed allegations of possible conflicting allegiances to both Israel and the United States. In 1956, Hadassah honored former Supreme Court justice and Zionist activist Louis Brandeis, and published this quote in its various local newsletters to convey to its members that although "ideals concerning Americanism, Zionism, and Patriotism are slightly confusing,"

> let no American imagine that Zionism is inconsistent with Patriotism... Every Irish American who contributed towards advancing home rule was a better man and a better American for the sacrifice he made. Every American Jew who aids in advancing the Jewish settlement in Palestine... will likewise be a better man and a better American for doing so. There is no inconsistency between loyalty to America and loyalty to Jewry.[41]

The newly established Sarah Kuzzy Hadassah chapter in Newark, New Jersey, appealed to Jewish women to get involved in Hadassah. In the local newsletter, the group published a list of questions and answers about Hadassah membership. One statement posed was "I am an American. My loyalty is here. Zionism means nothing to me." The answer to this question was that Hadassah members' loyalty as Zionists and Americans "makes us more patriotic because it makes us better citizens." The writer further argued that supporting a flourishing democracy like Israel in the Middle East was American.[42]

Continued support and activism in the United Nations remained a central aspect of Hadassah's political philosophy. Hadassah representatives served as liaisons to the United Nations, along with representatives from other NGOs. Members worked to strengthen UN foreign aid programs. Local chapters, such as the one in Portland, Oregon, organized public meetings with congressmen involved in the United Nations who spoke to members about the importance of UN work.[43]

THE STRANGER WITHIN

As tensions between Israel and its Arab neighbors rose, Arab nations, according to Hadassah leaders, bore the brunt of the blame for conflict in the Middle East and possible Soviet infiltration. Given Hadassah's history of seeking to maintain a culturally pluralistic society with equal rights for Arab citizens, Hadassah literature and rhetoric walked a fine line. On the one hand, it addressed the real political and security threat posed by Arab nations and their leaders, and, on the other hand, depicted Arabs living in Israel in more positive terms: All the while, it maintained that Arabs within Israel benefited from Israeli policy.

Hadassah's bifurcated views about Arab nations that depicted them as aggressors and the Arab population within Israel as worthy of rescue continued into the 1950s. Hadassah retained a largely progressive approach to the Arabs within Israel, which reflected a multicultural approach that had been adopted by Szold and other founders of the organization. However, at the same time, a hawkish and critical ideology about the Arab nations emerged.

Hadassah leaders continued to assure the membership that Arabs living in Israel would receive complete civil rights and would benefit from the new nation. An article published in the December 1950 issue of *Hadassah Newsletter*, entitled "No 'Jim Crow' in Israel: Arabs Enjoy Full Equality," briefed Hadassah members on the positive steps being taken to secure the success of Arabs in Israel: "Israel's Arab population is a prime concern of all government bureaus. The Israel Arab receives almost the same pay as his Jewish fellow worker and derives all the social benefits of the highly-developed Israeli society." The article went on to appeal to Hadassah's emphasis on child rescue by explaining that "thousands of illiterate Arab children went to school for the first time this year in compliance with the recently enacted Compulsory Education

Act."[44] Arab children under the care of the Israeli government, the article argued, received training in programs such as literacy "unheard of in the feudal societies of Israel's neighbors."[45] Their approach assured its members that not only would Arabs be protected from discrimination in Israel, but they would also actually have more promising futures.

Scores of articles published by Hadassah in the 1950s argued that Arabs thrived in Israel, even though their Arab brethren elsewhere attacked Israel's sovereignty. If a member had read all the articles dealing with Arabs in Israel in Hadassah publications in the 1950s, what they would have learned is that all possible measures were being taken to ensure Arab success in Israel. Arab and Jewish farmers worked together hand in hand: Arab women received vocational training, and the government even established an Arab kibbutz. Local newsletters, Hadassah meetings, and bulletins also provided information on Hadassah's equal treatment of Arab patients.[46]

The Israeli government, according to Hadassah publications, even went so far as to find homes for the many Arab refugees who had "lost their homes during the war."[47] Israeli Arabs, one article informed Hadassah members, also received a college education. According to another article, the issue of the success of Arabs within Israel should retain significance for the Jewish community the world over. "The question of the Arab minority in Israel touches on a tender nerve in the consciousness not only of Israel itself but of Jews the world over." The article, however, dissuaded Jews from drawing a parallel between the Jews of the diasporic Jewish experience with anti-Semitism and the Arab situation in Israel. Instead, it suggested that the Arabs in Israel experienced an almost familial program of cultural uplift. Jewish suffering, the author argued, stemmed from Christian anti-Semitism, "a social and mental aberration of the gentile world." Through their anti-Semitism, gentiles blocked Jews from having access to their institutions. But "Jews always maintained a high level of culture and social adaptability." Jews thus bore the brunt of anti-Semitism in spite of their advanced cultural and economic status. Arabs in Israel, the author contended, "have a population with a much lower economic and social standard than those of the majority of the state, a population which is part of the Arab peoples of the Middle East."[48] The economic and social standards of the Arab population needed to be "raised" to that of the Jewish population. The piece reflected a dichotomy between the desire of Hadassah members to safeguard the rights of Arabs in Israel and Hadassah's perception that Arabs were in need of Westernization, Jewish charity, and social uplift.

Hadassah information on the issue of Arabs in Israel often mirrored the public relations material published by the Israeli government. In a 1955 publication entitled "The Arabs in Israel," the Israeli government detailed how Arabs in Israel maintained a better standard of living and had more economic and educational opportunities in Israel than in the past or in any contemporary Arab country: "The standard of living of the Arab peasants in the country is today higher than at any previous time and in any other Middle Eastern country."[49] This ninety-two-page publication provides a glowing report on the fair and equal treatment of Arabs in Israel and on their successful acculturation.

Hadassah literature often repeated the findings of the Israeli government, about the high standard of living of Arabs in the Middle East in comparison with the rest of the Arab world and the fact that more than 80 percent of Arab farmers living in Israel worked and owned their own land.[50] Israel, unlike other Arab nations, granted Arab women in Israel full suffrage and Arabs had representation in the Israeli Knesset (parliament).[51] Hadassah literature continued to inform its members that Arabs received equal access to medical service even during times of warfare such as the Suez crisis when, "arrangements were made for a sick Arab girl to cross the Israel-Jordan frontier in order to obtain Hadassah's medical help."[52]

In 1958, Leon Uris's epic novel about the establishment of Israel took the American Jewish community by storm. The issue of Zionism so central to Hadassah's mission entered the public imagination on a mass media scale through the book and later film. Hadassah local chapters invited Uris as a guest speaker.[53] *Exodus* weaves the stories of Jewish refugees from the Holocaust who make Aliyah to Palestine in 1947. As Deborah Dash Moore has shown, the film version presented a romantic version of "Frontier Zionism" that remains as part of the public imagination today.[54] Another form of Zionism is also presented, "muscular Zionism," a form of Zionism that sought not only to establish the state of Israel but also to identify Jewish men with masculine traits such as militarism and aggressiveness.[55]

The book *Exodus* painted a fairly simplistic portrait of Arab-Jewish relations in Palestine. Jewish men take up arms, in this novel, to protect the new Jewish homeland. According to the novel, these aren't your stereotypical "Jew boys" emasculated by the tragedy of the Holocaust. As Kitty says of the protagonist, Ben Canaan, "Well, I'll say one thing. This Ben Canaan doesn't act like any Jew I've ever met. You know what I mean. You don't particularly think of them in a capacity like his... or fighters... things of that sort."[56] The book had particular significance for Hadassah members because one of the central characters, the young Holocaust refugee Karen, lives in Gan Dafna, a Hadassah Youth Aliyah camp.

As the 1950s drew to a close, the United States stood poised to enter the 1960s as a world superpower engaged in interventionist Cold War politics. Simultaneously, domestic issues of racial inequality, women's subjugation, and a general questioning of once-held assumptions about the American government boiled up to the surface, dramatically changing notions of acceptability and political action for people throughout America. Through Hadassah, Jewish women tackled the shifting sands of the 1960s social revolution by once again adapting their message and action toward new trends.

CHAPTER III

JEWISH AMERICAN WOMEN IN ACTION: HADASSAH MEMBERS AND POLITICAL ENGAGEMENT IN DOMESTIC ISSUES IN THE 1950S AND 1960S

While some may be familiar with Hadassah's political and philanthropic efforts to support the state of Israel, an often neglected but essential aspect of Hadassah's work focused on domestic policy and politics. Hadassah educated and engaged thousands of Jewish American women in the 1950s and 1960s on domestic issues such as civil rights and civil liberties, immigration reform, and the Great Society legislation.

As an important political and philanthropic outlet for Jewish American women, Hadassah engaged in a variety of political activities in the 1950s and 1960s. This political activity required women to be active in this arena at a time when hegemonic gender norms dictated that they remain at home and tend to their families.

Hadassah reached its members with information on domestic politics through conventions, meetings, social functions, fashion shows, pamphlets, and publications. Hadassah members received Hadassah publications, including *Hadassah Magazine* or *Hadassah Newsletter*. They constituted the "largest single subscription group of any Anglo-Jewish publication in the world."[1] *Hadassah Magazine*, which replaced *Hadassah Newsletter* in 1960, boasted a readership of over one million.

In the postwar era, a constant barrage of Cold War rhetoric, espoused by mainstream media and politicians, warned Americans of the danger of the nuclear threat. In this rhetoric, the Communists threatened not only American dominance on the geopolitical level but also the very fabric of American society. Anxiety over the Soviets reached extreme proportions and in part created an atmosphere of hysteria that lent itself to the devastating politics of accusations and personal destruction called McCarthyism.

The political ideology of McCarthyism sought to identify and destroy Communism and Communist sympathizers in America.[2] Many liberal organizations worried about being targeted as Communist and about the solvency of their own organizations. Women's organizations in particular were targeted by McCarthyites, and organizations like the AAUW almost disintegrated because of internal divisions on the issue.[3]

As chapter 2 demonstrated, in its attempt to increase support for Israel by the United States, Hadassah leaders utilized a Cold War geopolitical argument that demonized Communism while championing Israel as a stable democracy in the region.[4] At the same time, their domestic rhetoric often challenged the anti-Communist mentality by arguing against McCarthyism either openly or subtly and by aligning themselves with liberal causes, such as the civil rights movement, that were often associated with un-Americanism by anti-Communist ideologues.

MCCARTHYISM

The American Affairs Committee of Hadassah was specifically devoted to addressing domestic political issues. The American Affairs Committee and local chapter members engaged in American Affairs projects, which included efforts to educate members and the community on the importance of voting and supporting the United Nations. The Hadassah American Affairs Committee represented American Jewish women's voices on domestic issues. At Hadassah's annual convention in San Francisco in 1950, American Affairs included in its mandate the "education and dissemination of information on such matters as civil liberties."[5] Articles and speeches published by Hadassah dealt with freedom of speech or civil liberties by explicitly or implicitly alluding to the McCarthyite purge.

Invited guest and Columbia University history professor Henry Steele Commager spoke at the thirty-seventh annual Hadassah convention in 1951 in Atlantic City of the dangers of McCarthyism. He argued that the United States must "vindicate its newfound position" of world dominance because of the victory in Korea by "destroying McCarthyism and all that it symbolizes" on the domestic front.[6]

Figure 2. Hadassah Convention, Philadelphia, 1957.
Photo by G. D. Hackett, courtesy of Hadassah, The Women's Zionist Organization of America.

In addition, Commager concluded also that the United States must align itself with the United Nations and act within the international community. Referring to both McCarthyism and Cold War politics abroad, Commager stated, "We must set our own house in order and see to it that we, who preach democracy and equality and justice and tolerance, practice these things at home and abroad."[7]

Writer and scholar Howard Mumford Jones, in an article published in *Hadassah Newsletter* in 1953, pointed out to Hadassah members valid reasons for fearing that "bigotry" threatened America in the form of McCarthyite rhetoric and actions:

> Such reasons might be found in any newspaper or radio or television program... We are all too familiar with the behavior of Congressional

committees; with the way persons have been dropped from the nation's services — civil or military — on the suspicion of being under suspicion.[8]

He explained that Communists in fact only made up "less than one-fifteenth" of the U.S. population and that the "hysteria" was a vast overreaction. He also contended that the psychology of fear that had emerged from the "bigotry" of the Red Purge weakened the nation.[9]Hadassah passed a resolution, in 1954, proposed by the American Affairs Committee that further stressed the organizations' objections to McCarthyist rhetoric. Again, the language referred to civil liberties and the constitution. After acknowledging the dangerous threats of the times, such as the "atomic warfare," the resolution stated that Hadassah rejected the politics of fear.[10] In this new resolution, Hadassah linked Judaism and Americanism with freedom:

> To equate nonconformity with disloyalty; to whittle away the inalienable rights guaranteed to all Americans by their Constitution in the name of defending that instrument; to bar the concept of free enterprise from the realm of ideas is to betray our past and endanger our future. Freedom to pursue the truth, to exchange ideas, and to disagree with accepted opinion are the freedoms which have made America great and represent its proudest possession. The American tradition of freedom is also the Jewish tradition. In these days of understandable anxiety, we, as Americans and as Jews, must reforge the links which bind us to the great ideals of freedom bequeathed to us by our forbears. Civil Liberties are the foundation of this freedom and constitute the most powerful weapon against totalitarianism and tyranny.[11]

Throughout 1954 and after, many instructional articles published in *Hadassah Newsletter* explained to members the history and importance of civil liberties. These articles explicitly attacked the Red Purge as hurtful to American freedom and ideals. In January 1954, an article entitled "Anatomy of the Fifth Amendment" painted a hypothetical scenario where a "liberal professor" accused of "being a Communist" refuses to answer on the grounds of the Fifth Amendment so as to not incriminate himself. The article proceeded to instruct readers on the history of the constitution and the importance of the Fifth Amendment. The article attempted to provide a fuller understanding of the legal, political, and personal reasons one might use the Fifth

Amendment and, therefore, that its use should not be taken as an indication of guilt.[12]

Hadassah pushed its stance on civil liberties by publishing articles and promoting prominent political figures who challenged McCarthyism. Significant actors within the liberal community, such as the executive director of the American Civil Liberties Union, wrote articles in Hadassah publications condemning "Joseph McCarthy and his followers" and arguing that they threatened national security by "casting a blight on freedom of inquiry and communication" and creating a culture of fear that limited the capacity of the "Secretary of State to receive competent and honest reports."[13] The article provided a detailed outline of the various ways censorship had curtailed freedom of speech within the movie industry.

Often, Hadassah employed the rhetoric of politicians to bolster its policy choices. This was true both in the domestic stand against Cold War scapegoating and in efforts to depict Israel within a Cold War geopolitical context. Hadassah simultaneously borrowed from Cold War rhetoric on foreign policy issues and challenged it at home. Hadassah supporter and Republican congressman Jacob Javits subscribed to a similar political approach, and Hadassah often utilized his articles and speeches to legitimize their political stances. "A Congressman Looks at Congressional Investigations," Javits argues in this article that "the methods being currently used by some congressional committees greatly trouble millions of Americans who are sensible of our historic traditions of jurisprudence and who are concerned at the growing threat to our civil liberties."[14] He further criticized the way that "some Congressional investigations of subversive activities and Communists have turned, in effect, into prosecutions and penalties incurred — in a practical, if not in a legal, way — by those named in such investigations. These include the real possibility of loss of reputation, livelihood and standing in the community."[15] The next year, Javits gave a speech at a Hadassah fundraiser, warning of the dangers of Communism in the Middle East and the necessity of maintaining positive relations with Israel to bolster democracy in the region.[16]

This is a good example of the type of policy Hadassah employed: on the foreign affairs front they pushed for Jews and the American public to associate Israel with a prodemocracy stance in a bifurcated world. On the domestic scene, however, their American Affairs Committee, Hadassah leaders, and publications challenged McCarthyism and affiliated the organization with progressive agendas.[17]McCarthy's challenge to the U.S. Army in the McCarthy-Army hearings started a chain of events that led to the end of McCarthy's power. During the spring of 1954, America watched televised broadcasts of the hearings that made public McCarthy's attempt to weed out Communists within the army. This action seemed unwarranted in the eyes of many Americans. Now many politicians, particularly Republican moderates, began to criticize the participation of their party in "witch hunts" and attacks on civil liberties.[18] Building on this weakening of McCarthy's support in the Senate, Senator Ralph Flanders, a Republican senator from Vermont, led a successful campaign to censure McCarthy in 1954.[19]

The cover of *Hadassah Newsletter's* November 1954 edition hailed the weakening of the politics of fear associated with McCarthy. "During the year, there has been growing public recognition of the abuses of congressional investigating committees." Even Robert Oppenheimer, the famed scientist, lost his "security clearance," and this event had a shattering impact on the morale of scientists across the nation, the article argued. "One important gain has been recorded. For the first time in several years, McCarthy and his methods have been seriously challenged."[20] Although McCarthy himself lost power after the censure, McCarthy-like tactics and ideology still remained prominent in the United States, the article contended.

Hadassah leaders recognized the need to be vigilant on the issue of civil liberties. At the forty-first annual convention held in Chicago on November 2, 1955, concerns about censorship and McCarthy-like tactics still existed. Hadassah members and leaders remained wary that the ideology of McCarthy continued to pose a threat to "democracy." In a speech given at that conference, Buell G. Gallagher, president of the City College of New York, urged Hadassah members to accept that this was not "the time to relax." Gallagher argued that although some may think that "the victory for democracy within the United States" had been won, he was not so certain. He feared that with the demise of

McCarthy's power, "the first phase of hurricane zealot has passed over us, that we are presently in the calm of the eye of the storm." It was possible, in his opinion, that more incursions on civil liberties would follow. Indeed, freedom of speech and civil liberties remained an issue of interest to Hadassah throughout the 1950s, although the sense of urgency on the matter waned.[21]

IMMIGRATION

In addition to championing civil liberties through the work of its American Affairs Committee, Hadassah also worked to liberalize immigration quotas. The 1952 McCarran-Walter Act was one of the political issues that Hadassah chose to contest. An overhaul of the immigration system, the McCarran-Walter Act expanded the racist policy of relying on a national origins hierarchy in immigration laws. Immigrants hailing from northwestern Europe remained privileged, but the act also introduced a Cold War element to immigration law. Applicants would have to prove that they had no affiliation with any radical organizations. This requirement extended to naturalized citizens, who could be deported at any time if they were found to have suspicious associations.[22] The McCarran-Walter Act had anti-Semitic and anti-Asian overtones, since it privileged Northwestern European immigrants and barred entry to many Jews from Eastern Europe or anyone presumed to have radical affiliations at a time when Jews had been associated with leftist political movements. In addition, it continued a history of anti-Asian immigration policies that had started with the Chinese Exclusion Act of 1882.

Jewish groups, like the American Jewish Committee and the American Jewish Congress, sought to ameliorate the situation. Hadassah also worked through educating its membership and applying political pressure to repeal the act.[23] In the December 1954 edition of the *Hadassah Newsletter*, an article written by Ann Petluck, assistant executive director of the United Service for New Americans, argued for the repeal of the law. "What are the serious defects in the 1952 law? It is generally agreed among individuals and organizations working in the field of immigration that in many areas, contrary to American tradition, the law is not only decidedly illiberal but actually discriminatory against certain foreign national groups."[24] Petluck argued for acceptance of increased immigration as a positive asset to the American economy and outlined the limitations of the act. She also contended that "deportation should be forbidden," in all forms.[25]Hadassah's attack on the McCarran-Walter Act also reflected its anti-McCarthyist agenda. Senator Hubert H. Humphrey wrote an analysis of the status of liberalism in *Hadassah Newsletter*'s March 1953 edition entitled "The Crisis in Liberalism." Humphrey delineated an anti-McCarthy approach combined with severe criticism of immigration laws. Humphrey pointed to the contradictory policy of on the one hand fighting for freedom in the "Iron Curtain" while simultaneously blocking entry to the United States of foreign nationals from those areas. In addition, Senator Herbert H. Lehman warned Hadassah members of the "discriminatory" nature of the act:

> We should recognize, then, that our own immigration policy is a
> fundamental part of our international policy... while America has
> poured out billions of dollars in an effort to rebuild the free world and
> has sacrificed thousands of its sons on the battlefield in order to check
> Soviet aggression, we have affronted both our national heritage and the
> dignity of other peoples by the adoption of a discriminatory immigration
> law — the McCarran Act.[26]

Although President Truman vetoed the act, it passed by a House override of the veto. At that point, Truman established a commission on immigration and naturalization law. Hadassah representatives testified before that committee, arguing for an overhaul of the immigration policy that would allow more access to immigration and eradicate the act's Cold War overtones.[27]

In August 1953, the Eisenhower administration passed the Refugee Relief Act. It paid lip service to the criticisms of groups pushing for change within the system but failed to modify the existing laws in any significant way.[28] Hadassah continued to fight for expanded immigration and to educate its membership about the "unjust" nature of the McCarran-Walter Act throughout the 1950s.[29]

CIVIL RIGHTS

Jews and African Americans, longtime allies and sometime adversaries, swung the pendulum toward the side of camaraderie during the 1950s. Jews had a history of supporting organizations like the NAACP and the National Urban League through financial support and legal leadership. Among the forty-five members of the NAACP's first general committee, seven were Jews.[30] Historic ties between the Jewish and black communities strengthened dramatically in the post–World War II era and early civil rights era. Disclosure about the Holocaust brought to light the plight of both Jews and African Americans as targets for violence and extermination. Both communities understood the possibility that the virulence of hatred espoused by Nazis could easily transition into American culture. Many black soldiers rescued Jews from concentration camps in Europe, and both African American and Jewish soldiers worked toward the same cause of emancipation in WWII. In the aftermath of the war, it became increasingly clear that both anti-Semitism and racism remained problems within the United States.[31] Jews and African Americans formed a loosely knit alliance to protect civil rights and racial understanding within the United States. Cultural pluralism, already part of Hadassah ideology from its inception, now gained widespread acceptance among many Jewish groups, as well as African American organizations and many other liberal organizations.[32]

In 1954, the Supreme Court ruled in Brown versus the Board of Education of Topeka, Kansas, that both segregated schools and the doctrine of "separate but equal," was unconstitutional. Many groups and individuals challenged the legitimacy of the Supreme Court ruling and ignored the mandate or fought against it. In this atmosphere, Hadassah's fortieth annual convention meeting in 1954 adopted this resolution endorsing desegregation:

> Hadassah, The Women's Zionist Organization of America, together with men and women everywhere who believe that democracy rests on basic truths — that among these truths is the doctrine of the equality of all men — hereby acclaims the decision of the supreme court of the United States banning racial segregation in public schools in America; and goes on record as welcoming this decision as evidence of the vitality

of democracy in America and of the identification between democratic theory and practice.[33]

None could doubt that Hadassah stood squarely in favor of desegregation. Hadassah's long history of incorporating cultural pluralism and multicultural acceptance had established an attitude toward racism that only strengthened throughout the 1950s to lead Hadassah to align itself with the civil rights movement.[34]

Hadassah incorporated the emphasis on civil rights into its American Affairs program and also ran multiple informative articles in support of the issue of desegregation. In June 1954, one month after the Supreme Court decision on school desegregation was passed in May, the *Hadassah Newsletter* ran an article by Channing H. Tobias, then chairman of the board of directors of the NAACP and a former U.S. delegate to the United Nations. The article ran on the cover page, with an accompanying photo of two girls, one white and one black, facing each and other holding hands. The title of the article was "United We Stand; Supreme Court Ends School Segregation."[35]

Hadassah members read that this decision "was the most important single step forward for the Negro-American since the ratification, in 1870, of the Fifteenth Amendment, which removed the color ban from the ballot."[36] Channing, in effect, extended an invitation for Hadassah members to participate more fully in the smooth implementation of desegregation and of other efforts of the NAACP. While explaining the impact and history of segregation on American citizens, Channing also outlined ways in which "law abiding citizens who are anxious to translate this decision into a program to eradicate racial segregation in public schools" could participate in the acceleration and successful implementation of the ruling by lobbying their "local school boards" and school officials.[37] He emphasized that all Americans "who value our Hebraic-Christian heritage of human brotherhood" and who wished to maintain American's position as the leader of the "free world" should celebrate the victory gained by the Supreme Court decision.[38]

The American Affairs Committee continued to stress civil rights in its annual report from September 1955 to September 1956. The chairman, Mrs. Epstein, wrote: "The American Affairs Committee of Hadassah was increasingly concerned during the past year with those problems of which all freedom-loving Americans are conscious. The change in the climate with respect to civil rights has not dulled the alertness of groups and agencies organized for the purpose of preserving American freedoms." The report goes on to note that the Supreme Court judgment on desegregation had been met with tremendous opposition in the South and that Hadassah supported the Supreme Court judgment as "the law of the land."[39] Several articles charted advancements and struggles facing civil rights legislation, while American Affairs literature kept members informed of developments.[40] Local chapters held information sessions about civil rights issues.[41] Hadassah chapters in the South learned that American Affairs projects "relates to three main areas — civil rights and civil liberties, American foreign relations in the United Nations."[42]

In 1958, at a convention at which prime minister of Israel Golda Meir spoke, Hadassah adopted an additional civil rights resolution. This resolution challenged members to commit themselves "through a program of positive education to the endeavors of dispelling fear and hate from our midst, preventing subterfuges and evasions which lead to the disobedience of the law of the land and of counteracting violence by obedience to the laws of our country."[43] The resolution further reiterated recognition of the Supreme Court decisions on civil rights matters as "the final authority in the interpretation of the constitution." While all people have the right to criticize the Supreme Court, according to the resolution, "that right of criticism does not carry within it disobedience to or circumvention of the law." Lastly, the resolution stated that Hadassah members believe that most Americans "recognize and hold these principles to be ethically and morally sound."[44]

American Affairs literature and activities also encouraged Hadassah members to register and vote for both local and national elections. In some cases, this need to vote was directly tied to the civil rights issue. Belle C. Davis, chair of the Mount Vernon chapter of Hadassah American Affairs in New York, organized a Hadassah event where Republican and Democratic candidates for the Twenty-sixth Congressional District outlined their platform on what she considered were the two key issues for Hadassah members' national foreign policy and civil rights. Members were encouraged to bring their husbands and friends to this event to get the word out about the vote.[45] Belle Davis wrote an article pleading with Hadassah members to vote to influence the major issues of day, including desegregation, by the "intelligent use of our personal vote."[46] Hadassah chapters competed with one another to see how many voters they could register. The Hadassah Shoreline chapter in Chicago pledged forty-five members to participate in a voter registration drive for 100 percent voter registration, "in order to beat the claim of Wausau, Wisconsin, of being the first in nation to reach this goal."[47]

In the South, Jews' position as outsiders and targets for anti-Semitic hostility placed Jews in a precarious position. Many shied away from participating in civil rights action because of this tension, while some tried to make gestures toward the black community by serving black clients and occasionally hiring African American workers. Some Jews did make public their support for civil rights and became activists and later targets for hostility. A wave of bombings directed at Jewish community supporters of civil rights swept the South between 1954 and 1959. Referring to the bombing of a synagogue in Atlanta, Hadassah passed a resolution condemning these "acts of intimidation" designed to silence the "vast majority of law-abiding Americans." The dynamite planted at these centers, according to the resolution, was aimed not only at destroying buildings but also at the destruction of "the moral and ethical principles which emanate from these centers, and therefore, at the basis of our democracy." The resolution further urged that "no effort be spared" in the investigation in order to find who was responsible for these crimes and bring the perpetrators to justice.[48] In the 1960s, Hadassah encouraged members to view themselves as activists with a political mission. The 1960s, however, presented a potent challenge to this spirit of collaboration as Black Nationalism and separatism, popularized by the 1964 publication of Malcolm X's autobiography and by activists such as Stokely Carmichael, threatened Jewish notions of acceptable forms of protest and ideology.[49] Nonetheless, particularly in the early 1960s, Jewish men and women remained active in the civil rights movement. They participated in freedom rides, in the SNCC activity, and a variety of other civil rights activities.[50]

Hadassah continued, throughout the 1960s, to advocate for civil rights legislation and more determined efforts to desegregate the

South. Yet anxieties over Black Nationalism caused Hadassah members and leaders to question the relationship of Jews and blacks and to fight even further to maintain what they saw as the least threatening ways to collaborate with the black community.

The strengthening of civil rights remained a central mandate of the American Affairs branch of Hadassah during the 1960s. Among the various responsibilities of the appointed Washington representative of the national board that served as a liaison between Hadassah's American Affairs program and the Washington, DC political community was the maintenance of ties and information regarding civil rights.[51]

Articles in *Hadassah Newsletter* and *Hadassah Magazine* educated Hadassah members about the difficult attempts made to combat segregation in the South. These articles described sit-ins and freedom rides in positive terms. One article, entitled "Civil Rights Report: The Momentum of History Is Working against Segregation," was accompanied by picture of a sit-in, with smiling activists juxtaposed with a picture of Martin Luther King at a NAACP meeting. The caption read, "Renowned leader of the Negro struggle for civil equality, reiterates his faith in the ultimate triumph of justice at a NAACP convention." It further read, "Below, confident of the moral rightness of their demands, militant young Negro students smilingly brave insult and possible violence in 'sit-in strike,' one of the many protests that characterized the Negro's mood in 1961."[52] Several articles such as this one detailed the history and progress of desegregation. Hadassah had officially supported desegregation in their resolution. Had this just been a face value attempt to support desegregation, they could have stopped at that; however, throughout the 1950s and the 1960s, Hadassah continued to support civil rights activity.

The Philadelphia chapter cochairs of the American Affairs Committee told their members, "It is important that we be aware of what is going on. The Civil Rights and Civil Liberties issues, Freedom Riders, and human relations law, and Fair Educational Opportunities Act, may not be a part of the first session of the Ninety-seventh Congress, but they will come up. Let us be properly informed and learn to do our share."[53] That same year, at Hadassah's midwinter conference, resolutions were passed and publicized in Hadassah material, "supporting the advancement of civil rights and civil liberties so that every citizen will enjoy the rights and privileges guaranteed by the constitution."[54]

Ruth Gruber Michaels penned the ongoing *Hadassah Newsletter* and magazine column "Dairy of a Jerusalem Housewife" or "Diary of an American Housewife," depending on where she was reporting from. In her long-lived column, Gruber Michaels invited Hadassah readership into her home as she covered political issues as well as discussed personal family issues.

In her article "Desegregation in the South: Progress Is Visible, But Not Yet Won," Ruth Gruber Michaels charted a recent speaking trip she made to several southern cities and local Hadassah chapters. She gave an eyewitness account of the limitations of desegregation and what she called "a token integration." After explaining some of the "small battles" she witnessed in the area of integration on her trip, Michaels explained, "These, however, are still small victories. Years of agony lie ahead in the North as well as the South. Let no one think 250 years of slavery and 100 years of degradation can be erased overnight."[55] Michaels used strong language to convey her message; she wrote about slavery as a crucial historical issue often left out of discussions of racism in America. Michaels warned of the growing power of the white supremacist movement led by George Wallace. In one article, she provided quotes from local southerners that equated Wallace with "McCarthy" and credited him with constructing "a regular Gestapo in Alabama." Michaels also pointed out that the "racists" were also often "anti-Semites."[56] Thus, with the friendly and familiar voice of an "American housewife," Ruth Gruber Michaels affirmed strong support for the civil rights movement and a rejection of racist attitudes.

Later that same year, Ruth Gruber Michaels wrote another eyewitness account, this time of her participation in the historic march on Washington on August 28, 1963. At that event, Martin Luther King Jr. seared into the national consciousness his famous "I have a dream" speech. In her article, Michaels described a historic march with 210,000 people — "the greatest demonstration this capital has seen since the birth of the Republic."[57] Michaels depicted a joyful occasion where families marched together — Jews, Christians, whites, and blacks — all as one. The Jewish perspective remained a central theme in the report, with quotes from various rabbis and Jewish officials who had participated in the march. A mainstream picture of Jewish support was thus presented to Hadassah readers, introducing once again civil rights activism as a Jewish activity. Rabbi Marc Tannebaum was quoted in the article as saying, "Had this march taken place in the 1930s in Germany, there might never have been the mass murder of Jews. The conscience of Christians might have been awakened as our consciences are being awakened today."[58] Hadassah members again heard one of their own reporting to them the efforts of Jews to help others being oppressed as they had been.

Responding to a conference called by Vice President Johnson in July of 1963, in order to rally support for his Civil Rights Bill, Hadassah president wrote a letter declaring the organization's support of the effort. She explained that the "National board of Hadassah representing 318,000 members... Voted unanimously to help mobilize favorable public opinion on behalf of the administration's Civil Rights Bill."[59] To put this vote into action, Hadassah members at the 1963 convention voted to adopt a new civil rights resolution, endorsing and supporting the Civil Rights Bill. The resolution stated that the "program is in full accord with Hadassah's traditional position on Civil Rights." In addition, the resolution urged members to lobby political officials in their community to pass this legislation.[60] In its 1964 national conference, Hadassah renewed its support for the bill by calling on the federal government to ensure that guarantees of equality would be enforced regardless of "color, race or country of origin." The statement further urged Hadassah members to engage in "active participation with your respective boards of education, commerce, industries, enterprises, and institutions in your community, thereby striving to bring about a true equity of opportunity in all areas mentioned in this civil rights bill."[61]

In 1964, Johnson's Civil Rights Bill passed, but the South experienced more race-related violence with the bombing of a church in Selma, Alabama. Hadassah again lent support to the passage of the new Civil Rights Bill and harshly condemned the bombing in Selma. In a briefing sent to American Affairs chapter heads and meant for dissemination to chapter members, the Hadassah American Affairs national department wrote, "It is because the present aim of the Negro people in these areas strikes more deeply into the corrupt structure of law enforcement and legal power than have their previous efforts, that it has provoked violent ripostes."[62] The briefing further explained that segregation still remained a force to be reckoned with in many parts of the South. Positive strides resulting from sit-ins and the Civil Rights Bill of 1964 only offered "the first basis for tangible gain." Securing the unimpeded ability to vote, "which is as forbidden to some southerner Negroes as it was to their pre-Civil War forebears — strikes at the heart of the matter."[63] At Hadassah's national convention in 1966, held in Boston, Massachusetts, Hadassah delegates adopted a resolution supporting the Civil Rights Act of 1966 and reaffirmed their commitment to the expansion of civil rights.[64]

BLACK POWER

While Hadassah built on its civil rights tradition by working with black organizations, a new shift in the civil rights movement toward Black Nationalism and black power, sometimes interpreted as separatism, created a strained relationship between Jewish liberal organizations and the black community.[65] Black Nationalist leaders such as Stokely Carmichael attracted many black northerners who felt alienated from the Southern civil rights movement. In addition, the emergent emphasis on pan-Africanism on the part of many Black Nationalists and their critique of colonial oppression in Africa gradually shifted allegiance in many parts of the black community away from Zionism. Thus, they aligned themselves with the Palestinian and Arab third world as opposed to Israel, now seen by some as a colonialist first world country.[66]

Fears about black power and the questioning of Zionism produced anxiety among the ranks of Hadassah. At the 1968 Hadassah national convention, Whitney M. Young Jr., executive director of the National Urban League, told Hadassah members that the black power movement provided positive qualities to the black community and that the Urban League supported black "pride and self-respect." But he also warned that the separatist strain should not be tolerated. Young also stated that white people were in the greatest position of power to change the racist system from within, as opposed to relying on the black community to champion the cause; thus, he supported civil rights action.[67]

Hadassah published statements by Martin Luther King Jr. in an article honoring the "testament of Martin Luther King Jr.," which clearly rejected black power. In an excerpt from a speech given to the Jewish Rabbinical Assembly in March 1968, King was quoted as saying that he regretted "that the slogan 'Black Power' ever came into being." He further commented that "it has become confusing and so often promotes Black domination rather than Black equality."[68] King also expressed the conflicted view toward Jews. "For they see Jews both as an ally in the civil rights movement but also as economic oppressors abusing their power as landlords within the ghetto."[69]

Further fueling the fires of fear, Robert Gordis, a professor of religion at Temple University, wrote a scathing critique of the black separatist movement in an article published in *Hadassah Magazine*. After the death of Martin Luther King Jr., black separatism had become the dominant voice in the black community, he claimed. One aim of black separatists, he explained, was to create "all Negro Ghettos," ridding the communities of the "white businessman." The communities would be equipped with all-black police departments, fire departments, and school systems. If this came to pass, Dr. Gordis cautioned Hadassah members, "In a few years our public schools will have produced cadres of black racists consumed with hatred for all non-blacks and as disruptive of the social order and destructive of themselves as the German Nazis in their heyday."[70] One can see how an atmosphere of fear was nurtured through articles like these and the wider media's depiction of Black Nationalism. A new breed of "Nazi," according to Gordis, could be developing within the American culture.

In an effort to present an explanation of the complexities within the black community and to put a positive spin on Hadassah efforts for civil rights and its alliance with the black community, an American Affairs kit was sent to American Affairs representatives as a guide for understanding current events. One section entitled "Civil Rights Legislation" provided a question and answer form and an explanation of goals to be accomplished through association with "moderate" civil rights groups. Hadassah therefore continued to push for civil rights legislation and align itself with what saw as the moderate wing of the black community. Hadassah members learned that just as the white community had divisions between "moderates," "conservatives," and "radicals," so too was the black community divided. Among the efforts outlined as moderate areas of civil rights that would be supported by Hadassah were advances in: housing, education, medical treatment, employment, and "adequate income for those unable to work to live with self-respect."[71]

In a similar kit produced by the American Affairs Committee on February 17, 1969, a section entitled "Black Organizations" provided several pages of analysis of the black community and civil rights groups. Hadassah members were encouraged to view the black community as diverse, with many groups supporting integration, including organizations like CORE, the NAACP, and the Urban League. The Black Panthers and SNCC were characterized as nonintegrationist and negative groups promoting violence and "confrontation."[72]

Although threatened by Black Nationalism and a growing sense of frustration and even anti-Semitic undertones in some branches of the black community, Hadassah continued to support the passage of civil rights legislation. In a resolution passed at the February 1969 midwinter national convention, Hadassah members condemned anti-Semitism within the black community. The same resolution, however, urged Hadassah members to "continue its vigorous participation in all efforts to assure the realization of the American ideal of freedom and justice for all."[73] The same year, Hadassah passed a resolution on desegregation protesting the delayed process of integration in the South and urging the federal administration to assist in the "speedy implementation of full school integration."[74]

Hadassah leaders found ways to negotiate the crisis between the Jewish and black community in the late 1960s. Choosing to dismiss what they viewed as the negative constructions of Black Nationalism as irrelevant, they aligned themselves with "moderate" voices. Instead of just breaking ties with the black community and divorcing themselves from civil rights action, they chose to be selective in their approach to civil rights and to continue to work in that area. Even amid a flood of perceived black anti-Semitism, Hadassah leaders and members worked to maintain a relationship with officials in the black community deemed responsive to their efforts.

Alongside its support for civil rights, Hadassah also endorsed and lobbied on behalf of Johnson's Great Society efforts. These consisted of a series of social welfare and economic programs meant to eradicate "poverty and racial injustice."[75] At Hadassah's annual 1967 conference, the organization endorsed a statement in which it stated its approval of Johnson's antipoverty program: "The passage of this bill will be a first step toward giving every citizen an opportunity to share in America's material abundance and in the cultural, social, common, and political life of the country."[76] Hadassah reiterated its support for Great Society programs like Medicare, the antipoverty act, and the revision of the restrictive immigration laws in a statement adopted at its 1966 midwinter national conference.[77] In a resolution addressing antipoverty legislation adopted at Hadassah's annual national conference in September of 1967, the organization urged Congress to provide adequate funding in order to ensure the success of the "War on Poverty."[78] The American Affairs Committee produced several kits that dealt with the issues of the War on Poverty and various other initiatives within the realm of housing, medical aid, and hunger relief programs. The kits were designed to educate members about the problems facing Americans, and they wholeheartedly supported efforts by the Johnson administration to remedy the situation.[79] While Hadassah members certainly played an important role in their lobbying and philanthropic activities in support of Israel, they also engaged in significant work at home. Through Hadassah, Jewish women learned not only about Israel but also about how to be effective and progressive American citizens. The relationship between this political action and hundreds of thousands of Jewish women is crucial to exploring the development of modern American Jewish women's identity.

'EMA' OR 'CONSCIOUS JEWESS': JEWISH MATERNALISM, ACTIVISM, AND GENDER ROLES IN THE 1950S

From the inception of Hadassah, its leaders sought consciously to carve out a space for Jewish women to participate in the male-dominated sphere of Zionism. In doing so, they developed an organization that emphasized practical work in Palestine as an avenue for American Jewish women to expand their sphere of influence and to grow as individuals.[1] Hadassah leaders encountered great hostility and criticism from the male leadership of the Zionist movement in the United States. Zionism, a political ideology often associated with masculinity and the formation of what Michael Berkowitz has called the "new Jewish man," left little room for women as equal participants in its ranks. Zionist leaders like Louis Lipsky embraced the marriage of masculinity and Zionism. An organization like Hadassah that was led by women challenged the importance of Zionism in his eyes and threatened to weaken the Zionist movement. Hadassah leaders fought to counter a myriad of criticism that they received from male-dominated Zionist groups and individuals who felt that Hadassah distracted from men's legitimate Zionist efforts.[2]

Borrowing from maternalist ideology, Hadassah leaders contended that, rather than engaging in ideological debates that produced little in the way of concrete assistance for Palestine, Jewish women possessed a unique drive to nurture that would be better expressed in practical ways.[3] In effect, Hadassah's top leadership was arguing that women as nurturers were actually doers and should emphasize this aspect of their personalities in their advocacy of the Zionist cause. Employing this rhetoric, Hadassah leaders constructed an ideology that allowed them to use ideals of maternalism to challenge gender norms. Women, they argued, were actually superior to men as Zionists because they cared more for the social welfare in Palestine and focused on the needs of the population rather than on political matters.[4] Eventually, male leaders such as Louis Brandeis would concur and see the value of Jewish women's participation in the movement.

In order to understand the developments of gender roles for Jewish women within Hadassah in the 1950s, it is crucial to appreciate the historical precedent that led up to this phenomenon. American Jewish women shook the foundations of Jewish religious and social life in the nineteenth and early twentieth centuries by introducing new innovations, such as mixed gender seating in synagogues, the feminization of synagogue membership, women as the central Jewish educators within the home, and the growth and increasing dominance of Jewish women-run charities and philanthropies.[5] Central to this new approach were shifting notions of gender and Jewish identity. The adoption by Jewish men and women of a Victorian ideal of female gentility and the moral superiority of women as mothers ironically acted as the catalyst for more women to participate in public discourse. Mainstream Victorian notions of womanhood merged with a traditional Jewish emphasis on the family and new expressions of the Judaic religious tenant of *tzedekah*, or righteous acts, to create new conceptions of Jewish womanhood.[6]

"German" middle-class Jewish women provided much of the impetus for the shifting gender norms in American Jewish culture. Spurred by the immigration of European Jews seeking to improve their situation economically, the number of Jews in America grew dramatically from 3,000 in 1820 to 240,000 in 1880.[7] Although traditionally thought of as primarily German émigrés, in reality, these Jewish immigrants also hailed from Poland, Bohemia, Moravia, Galicia, Alsace, Russia, and Lithuania.[8] The majority of these new "German" immigrants adapted well to life in America and attained the pecuniary advancements that had fed the mass migration. While poverty existed among the ranks of these early Jewish immigrants, as a whole, they moved relatively quickly into a middle-class status.[9]

As Jews moved up the economic ladder, they sought to emulate a set of Victorian ideals that included proscribed roles for men and women. Following their Christian neighbors, Jews elevated women's domesticity and their purportedly maternal nature to a new pinnacle. Within the realm of this new Jewish motherhood, women were ascribed new power as moral superiors. While this stance allowed women a voice within the community as esteemed mothers and wives, it negated the more traditional ideal of the Jewish woman as an economic participant within the family, who worked outside or inside the home so that her husband might study Torah.[10]

Mirroring genteel Gentile society, Jewish women used volunteerism as an avenue through which to maintain the Victorian gender ideal of domesticity while at the same time creating novel avenues for public female participation. In an action virtually unheard of in Jewish history, in the mid-nineteenth century in the United States Jewish women began organizing women's groups devoted to serious communal issues.[11] While men had been organizing in fraternal orders based on regional affiliation or synagogue issues, Jewish women gathered together for the first time to confront the serious social needs that had begun to emerge within the Jewish community.[12] Rebecca Gratz founded the first of these organizations, the Female Hebrew Benevolent Society, in Philadelphia in 1819; and by the mid-nineteenth century, similar women's Jewish organizations gained popularity across the country.[13] The bloodshed of the Civil War brought even more Jewish and non-Jewish women into the world of volunteerism as they worked to ameliorate the aftermath and harrowing conditions of battle through philanthropic and medical endeavors.[14]

While Jewish women were becoming well established in caretaker and charity roles, Jewish women also began to subscribe to precepts of the Victorian domestic model that stressed the importance of female education and women's role in spiritual life. In order for women to be true mothers capable of educating their children and uplifting the nation, they would have to be cultured and educated themselves.[15] In addition, Jewish women and men were aware of the feminization of Christian evangelical churches and sought to allow women more participation in a synagogue sphere that had previously been dominated by men.[16] Mixed gender seating in non-Orthodox synagogues, as opposed to segregated seating, marked a significant departure from previous gender roles.

Increasingly, Jewish women would come to dominate synagogue life, just as Protestant women were coming to dominate the church.[17] As the binary Victorian division of labor — women as the homemakers and men as the breadwinners — took hold within the Jewish community, women gained the responsibility for children's education in Judaism and Jewishness, an obligation once within the father's domain. As a result, Jewish education for women gained acceptance, and in 1838, Rebecca Gratz opened a Sunday school with an all-women staff that strove to educate Jewish girls, along with boys, in Jewish beliefs, scholarship, and traditions.[18]

By the late nineteenth century, many central European Jewish immigrants successfully advanced into the ranks of the middle class and beyond. In New York in 1890, for example, approximately 40 percent of Jews reported having a domestic servant and nearly 10 percent had several servants.[19]

At the same time that these Central European Jewish immigrants were experiencing high levels of social mobility, a new wave of nearly two million less-advantaged Jewish immigrants from Eastern Europe made their way to American shores, arriving between 1880 and 1914. Of the new population that emigrated from Galicia, Romania, and Russia, almost half were women.[20] The majority of these Eastern European women entered the ranks of the working class and created a culture of leisure and social exchange through dance hall attendance, movie going, and engagements with the new American consumer culture.[21] The new arrivals brought with them many cultural nuances that contributed to the Jewish community. Chief among those was an avid political activism and acceptance of Zionism that had been largely shunned by previous generations of American Jews.

Jewish women volunteered to aid the Eastern European newcomers and often worked to "uplift" their status.[22] Educated middle- and upper-class women were greatly influenced by the Progressive movement's emphasis on social service work and moral and economic uplift. In the early twentieth century, in addition to Jewish communal work, two new avenues for volunteerism captured the imaginations of Jewish volunteers: aid to immigrants and Zionism.[23]

In 1893, Hannah Solomon founded the first major Jewish women's organization, the National Council of Jewish Women (NCJW). The new organization provided middle- to upper-class Jewish women with a distinctively Jewish women's club that tackled Progressive reform issues such as social services for Eastern European immigrants, aid to the impoverished, and a campaign to abolish Jewish prostitution.[24] Relying heavily on a domestic ideology, the NCJW stressed the importance of women as mothers and celebrated the idea of a separate, maternal women's sphere as "divinely designed." Historian Faith Rogow has argued that while the NCJW provided women an avenue to voice their concerns, their acceptance of an ideology of domesticity "reaffirmed men's power rather than challenged it."[25] As with many women's clubs, NCJW followed a "pattern of conservatism."[26]

NCJW maternalism served as an important and high-profile model for Jewish womanhood, but its message nevertheless did not resonate with many women active in the Jewish community. While the NCJW held great clout and remained quite visible as an actor in American Jewish history, the organization's membership was at its height in 1950 of 100,000. This figure was dwarfed by the younger, more political Hadassah, which had a membership in 1950 of nearly triple that amount.[27]

A major component of NCJW's work reflected the Progressive movement's efforts to Americanize Eastern European Jewish immigrants. In a sometimes paternalistic manner, NCJW and non-Jewish progressives sought to assimilate the immigrant population into proper American culture. In contrast, Hadassah leaders such as Henrietta Szold actually admired the Eastern European immigrants, who had introduced her and other "German" Jews to Zionism.[28]

DOMESTIC IDEOLOGY

Hadassah maintained this leading role despite the challenges presented by competitors and by the Great Depression. By the 1930s, Jewish women looked to a variety of religious, charitable, or Zionist organizations — in addition to Hadassah and the NCJW — to which to volunteer their services and some in Hadassah feared that the new clubs might siphon off their membership. Groups such as the Organization for the Rehabilitation through Training (ORT), which worked to provide vocational education for Jews, greatly expanded. Local temple sisterhoods joined forces to create the national Federation of Temple Sisterhoods, which by 1928 had 55,000 members from over 300 synagogues.[29] Economic devastation also posed challenges to the extent to which women could or would volunteer their time. Many Jewish women took on additional economic responsibilities as they worked to reduce the impact of the economic downturn on their lives.[30]

During the 1940s and 1950s, the Jewish community in America experienced a period of complex socioeconomic, demographic, and ideological transformation. Although the psychological impact of the Holocaust had a major effect on the Jewish community, other factors also worked to change the environment for American Jews. Jewish earnings increased substantially due in part to postwar GI benefits (allotted to Jewish men who served in record numbers in World War II) and expanded educational opportunities, moving many working-class Jews, especially members of and descendants of the second generation of immigration, into a middle-class category.[31] As Karen Brodkin has argued, "Sons of working class Jews now went to college and became professionals themselves."[32] The wives of these sons also moved up in economic status. The postwar era also saw a dramatic increase in suburbanization among Jews. With home mortgages more easily accessible, more Jews moved out of the cities into the suburbs to own their own homes.[33]

Hadassah's appropriation of Americanism and the domestic ideal was in actuality part of an effort to cater to this wider array of members. However, domesticity and patriotism simultaneously and often ironically served to empower women who sought to challenge traditional gender roles and broaden their self-awareness. In many ways, the women of Hadassah encountered and created a complicated ideology that often stressed contradictory messages about the future of Jewish womanhood.

Hadassah incorporated much of this language of domesticity and the idea that women as mothers and wives could safeguard the nation emerged. Hadassah encouraged Jewish women to strengthen their identity as Jews. Although it stressed women's roles as homemakers, mothers, and wives, it simultaneously encouraged women to engage in political discourse and to challenge their husbands by devoting their time and energy to the cause and to educate themselves.

Many Jewish women in suburban postwar Jewish culture embraced the synagogue as the major source of their identity. However, much of the involvement of women in the temple sisterhood lacked the political and educational emphasis of an organization like Hadassah.[34] Women who joined groups such as Hadassah often were seeking ways in which to understand their place in the world as Jews, women, and Americans. Hadassah provided Jewish women with a voice of their own and empowered "Hadassah ladies" to work outside of the home by stressing their importance to political discourse in Israel and the United States, the Jewish community, and American democracy.

Messages that encouraged women to develop their minds and challenge husbands who would have rather had their wives at home were coupled with ones that stressed the domestic concepts of womanhood so prominent in the 1950s. In "This is Your Life," a brochure designed to inspire current members and recruit new members to Hadassah, the writer emphasized a restrictive suburbia-bound maternal role for women by stressing the essential contribution Jewish women made in transmitting Jewish culture to their children: "AS A JEW you have this duty: to safeguard the cultural and religious treasures of your people. This is part of your life in Hadassah." Hadassah backed up this call to Jewish mothers throughout its literature from this era by promising to educate women and provide them the essential tools needed for them and their children to embrace their Jewish heritage. Within the same brochure, however, women were urged to safeguard their liberties as educated American women and mothers and to keep in mind that their foremothers had historically lacked access to a Jewish education, let alone the right to serve as bearers of the cultural heritage:

> There have been times when men questioned your right to live by the teachings of your Jewish past. But in the United States, where strands from every corner of the earth are woven to make a democracy, your right is also your responsibility.[35]

The argument made in much of Hadassah's literature was that Jewish women had been given an opportunity to educate themselves and their fellow Jews on Jewish cultural history and proper forms of Jewish identity and that through Hadassah they could accomplish this goal and in the process become good American mothers.

Zionism also served as an avenue for an individual to express her mastery of Jewish heritage and identity and to connect to the generations of struggle in the past and the existing struggle in Israel. Hadassah offered women a message of empowerment: women — not men — had the power and the responsibility to educate themselves and others. This responsibility granted them the extension into the public sphere and also served to legitimate Jewish women's public and political expressions of their identity. However, these messages of empowerment often were coupled with more traditional notions of women's gender roles.

Jewish women's importance as maternal and cultural caretakers served as a legitimating principle for much of Hadassah rhetoric in the 1950s. An educated and active Jewish woman, Hadassah ideology expounded, could provide the proper education to her children. As neo-Victorian and new suburban notions of domesticity emerged during the 1950s, so too did the idea that Jewish mothers bore the responsibility to assure that Jewish cultural dissemination continued to be transmitted to future generations through children's education.

> What happens when you join Hadassah?... YOU BECOME A BETTER JEW... Examining your Jewish heritage, you learn your people's glorious heritage. You understand current problems better. You get a "perspective." Education through Hadassah gives you the basic certainties you need to live constructively and to guide your family toward a richer Jewish life.[36]

Through Hadassah, women could find a place for themselves within the Jewish community and create importance to their lives and that of their families. Indeed, Hadassah "Makes You Important" was a major slogan of the period. Brochures with a "June Cleaver" look-alike on the cover advertised that Hadassah offered more meaning to the life of the average housewife. Hadassah would make Jewish women important,

Figure 3. *Drawing from subject divider of Hadassah's 1957 "work kit," part of that year's "Mammoth Kit" manual for chapter leaders. Courtesy of Hadassah, The Women's Zionist Organization of America Inc.*

IMPORTANT BECAUSE... AS JEWS... Hadassah members declare, "we must safeguard the cultural and religious treasures of our people. Since this activity is intrinsic to Hadassah, we attract women of all ages themselves to be, and to make their children better Jews."[37]

Hadassah activism was thus legitimated by the fact that it helped to create better educated mothers with a strong sense of Jewish identity that could "safeguard the cultural and religious treasures of our people." While men were expected to be the breadwinners of the family, Jewish women's roles as Jewish educators, protectors, and mothers served as an excuse for women to leave the private sphere and engage in a range of political, social, and economic activities that ironically worked to challenge the domestic ideology of women's role within the home.

Education programs designed to strengthen Hadassah member's sense of Jewishness not only centered on Zionism but also included political awareness programs. In addition to political education, Hadassah members learned through panels and publications about Jewish history and holidays. Some local chapters even included a "Hadassah Prayer" in their yearbooks. This prayer asked G-d for guidance "in our task of aiding and providing for the spiritual needs of the community."[38] Hadassah programs ranged from Jewish education workshops on history and the Bible to studying Hebrew and explanations of holidays. Some chapters even held a "Jewish Home Beautiful" event. It showcased appropriate table settings for various Jewish holidays, while a member performed holiday songs.[39]

MATERNALISM

One of the most successful programs of Hadassah in the 1950s was the Youth Aliyah program. The maternal emphasis of Youth Aliyah—American club women helping disadvantaged foreign youth—served to attract new members. After Hadassah was named the official liaison for Youth Aliyah in America in 1943, its chapters increased in numbers from 272 to 375.[40] "Hadassah," one brochure argued, "is rescuing Jewish children from Arab lands and Iron Curtain countries through the Youth Aliyah movement which functions in 300 cooperative settlements and a network of special schools in Israel."[41] Articles and publications written about Youth Aliyah in Hadassah in the 1950s stressed the importance of women as nurturers and mothers and the need to protect Jews from anti-Semitism in all areas of the world, including the countries enclosed by the Iron Curtain.

Youth Aliyah invited Hadassah members to figuratively adopt a child in need. "WANTED A MOTHER EMA" (*ema* is the Hebrew word for "mother") was used in brochures designed to motivate American women to participate more fully in Youth Aliyah programming or to join Hadassah. Beside the caption in one such brochure was a picture of three children of varying ages. A short entry about each child explained his or her particular economic plight. The next page followed the same pattern and warned that "Jewish children and youth have become victims of political upheaval, discrimination, anti-Semitism." Through Youth Aliyah, American Jewish women could save these children from areas of the world like Eastern Europe and Arab lands with "Hitler-like economic and social persecution." America Jewish women were thus empowered by virtue of their responsibility as mothers of the Jewish people to "become a mother to a homeless child." [42]

Discussions of youth and children's programming thus carried messages about proper Jewish womanhood. Implicit in these messages was the notion that women naturally bear the responsibility for children by virtue of their maternal nature: "CHILDREN SUFFER AND YOU RESPOND. You know from your own children and those around you that there is no future for the world if any of the world's children is insecure." [43] Therefore, motherhood and womanhood predisposes women to have a greater appreciation for children. Although Hadassah in many ways challenged traditional gender norms by allowing women a political and public voice and by stressing the importance of women to Jewish cultural understanding, at the same time, it utilized traditional gender roles of the day that stressed the importance of women as the caretakers of the family. Rather than remaining in the private sphere, as Elaine Tyler May contends in her study of Protestant women, the Jewish family was encouraged to extend into the public sphere to publicly represent children, youth, the Jewish people, and Israel.[44]

Thus, a contradictory approach to gender was employed. On the one hand, it challenged restrictive notions about women's roles and, on the other hand, reinforced notions of domesticity. Jewish women, through Hadassah, were uniquely poised to rescue Jewish children and by extension Judaism itself from anti-Semitic hatred. "So through Hadassah," argued the literature, "you take on the sweetest task a woman can assume: you work for youth... Being a woman you also know that without love and unceasing vigilance, even a rescued child hurt by fear, poverty and orphan hood will not become a child again. So you watch and guide."[45]

Drives to raise money for other Hadassah activities such as its hospital fund also stressed the importance of programs that benefited children. An advertisement that ran in the *Hadassah Newsletter* showed a picture of a nurse caring for a sick child with a large caption: "IT'S YOUR CHILD TOO!" The ad went on to suggest that this child "in Israel is fighting for her life," and that Hadassah members could not stand by and not help. The advertisement further drew a parallel between the helpless and sick child and the state of Israel. "All Israel is engaged in a fight for 'life, liberty and the pursuit of happiness' today. And you are a part of it." Thus, Israel is equated within this text to a helpless child, with all of Hadassah serving as the responsible maternal caretaker.[46]

The emphasis on Hadassah's more traditional gender roles relied heavily on the extension of women's maternalism into the public sphere. Jewish women would be important not only to their own children but also to children all over the world, and they would care for a newborn nation of Israel. In Hadassah literature, very little emphasis was placed on the importance of women as wives.

While many of Hadassah's activities were geared toward its work in Israel, it also had many programs in the United States directed toward educating the youth in Hadassah values. Again, Hadassah members were to assume the responsibility for engaging American Jewish youth in Jewish cultural education and in Zionism as a vehicle for preserving Jewish identity. "As a woman your responsibility to youth is also basic for a fully rewarding way of life. So through your work for Zionist youth in this country, Hadassah makes it possible for you to 'connect' with the younger generation, among whom may be your children."[47]

References to patriotism infused Hadassah's gender discourse with another layer of meaning. "YOU ARE IMPORTANT BECAUSE it's Good Americanism: Hadassah members believe, 'we have not only responsibility but a duty to foster the democratic way of life at home and abroad... As American citizens, Hadassah women are expected to make up their own minds. We give them information to help them think. Their own zeal, intelligence and patriotism do the rest to keep them sensitive, responsive to their citizenship duties."[48] Good American women should be educated and take active civic, political, and cultural roles. Democracy and America itself worked to legitimate Jewish women's political and social action.

In fact, Hadassah literature not only argued that women should empower themselves, their children, and the Jewish community, but also that the entire world needed rescuing. Through education, action, and fund-raising, properly American "Hadassah ladies" would be well informed and well equipped for the challenge. "You BECOME A BETTER CITIZEN through Hadassah's American Affairs program. You receive information on the United Nations and on issues facing you as an individual American Citizen... Thus you are 'armed' to help protect democracy in the United States and foster freedom and justice elsewhere throughout the world."[49]

Hadassah also utilized education programs to define American Jewish womanhood to its members. Through Zionism and Jewish education provided by Hadassah, Jewish women would gain "importance" as better women, "better Americans, and better Jews." The culmination of Hadassah's work lay in the development of a woman who knew who she was, in addition to knowing her history and her political affiliation. Her Jewish identity could then successfully be handed down to the next generation of Jews:

> The Hadassah education program here is designed to give our members a sense of Jewish history and a high degree of responsibility for the continuing of a great tradition. It is not enough to be born Jewish — we must live as Jews. And we must give to our children the knowledge — the tools and the instruments — to make them want to live a positive Jewish life. It is not enough to pride ourselves on being the "People of the Book" — we must know these people and know this book. Pride in a great tradition can degenerate into complacency, unless we take seriously our responsibility for safe-guarding and re-interpreting the tradition. This implies knowledge, understanding and growth."[50]

While maternalism and Americanism acted as strong forces in the shaping of Hadassah women's identity and the platform of the organization, absent from the rhetoric was the domestic ideology of women's importance as wives. To the contrary, Hadassah women were instructed in ways to challenge their husband's authority and to demand respect for their activities through Hadassah. *Hands of Healing*, a promotional film released by Hadassah in 1951, detailed the experiences of one "Hadassah husband" as he visited Israel on a business trip after being "ordered by his wife," who works hard for Hadassah, "to take a look at my work too." While in Israel, "he has one of the greatest emotional experiences of his life."[51] He realized the importance of his wife's Hadassah work.

Hadassah husbands were encouraged to support their wives' activities. Movies were made and literature was written to introduce Hadassah husbands to Hadassah concepts and to defend their wives' right to participate in such a worthy cause. One Hadassah husband spoke of how his support for his wife had become "a career" in and of itself; it was a vehicle through which an everyday businessman was able to expand beyond the realm of his daily work life:

> It has been my privilege to address many evening meetings of Hadassah chapters, and always there is a goodly sprinkling of Hadassah Husbands. Their very presence tells a story — a story of mutual participation with their wives in being part of this great movement."[52]

A Hadassah husband would have to follow the lead of his wife or at the very least "look upon his wife with respectful puzzlement" and think to himself, "How did this housewife become so knowledgeable in international affairs, so able a defender of civil rights?"[53] Hadassah women thus challenged the dominant and traditional gender norms of the day that defined women as mothers and housewives and occasionally made husbands the passive spectators in their lives.

Hadassah women's conceptions of womanhood differed from those studied by May, who saw the private sphere as the only acceptable arena for women's activity in the rhetoric of the 1950s. While Hadassah may have used concepts of motherhood to defend and legitimate their cause, they simultaneously challenged the foundations of the domestic ideology of the 1950s. In relation to Jewish women's roles as housewives, the organization espoused a gender consciousness that sought to gain respect — and deference — from their husbands.

Hadassah introduced Jewish American women to a form of gender consciousness that incorporated traditional notions of maternalism in order to empower women to channel their maternal authority into new male-dominated territory such as politics, Jewish education, and Zionism. At the same time, women were encouraged to see themselves as breaking new ground as women. On the Jewish cultural front, they would take on the role of cultural disseminators once attributed to men. Unlike the women of the past, who were described as concerned primarily with beauty and pleasing men, Hadassah urged women to respond to "modern society's" new approach to gender roles. In an article published in 1958, entitled "Who Is She? An Appraisal of the Composite of the Hadassah Member," Hadassah members are told, "For the social revolution of the last century has placed women on a more or less equal footing in the competitive world and has moved her to the forefront of organized communal life."[54] The typical Hadassah woman shared in this social revolution. The article expands that she is "fascinating, aggressive, knowledgeable," and, most important, she no longer defines herself as only a wife. She realizes that a "shrinking physical world has expanded her original purpose from companion of man to companion of mankind." Thus, Hadassah women, we are told, shared in this new uniquely 1950s form of womanhood with "an added ingredient — a deep consciousness of her Jewish roots." The Hadassah woman represented the quintessential modern twentieth-century "emancipated woman."[55] "And so, the question is answered, who is she? Can be answered with: She is an alert daughter of the 20th century, she is a conscious Jewess — and a soldier."[56] Hadassah women are thus equated both with progressive values and with a warriorlike presence. Hadassah women figuratively served as warriors for Jewish women and for Israel.

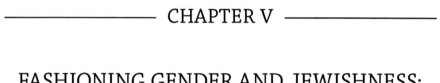

CHAPTER V

FASHIONING GENDER AND JEWISHNESS:
HADASSAH, FASHION SHOWS, AND BEAUTY
CULTURE IN THE POST–WORLD WAR II ERA

In fall 1958 at the Hotel Fontainebleau in Miami Beach, Florida, 2,500 Jewish women representing 315,000 Hadassah members from all over the United States converged at the yearly Hadassah convention. The keynote speaker at the event was none other than current foreign minister and future prime minister of Israel, Golda Meir, who would become one of the first women to lead a democracy in modern world history. At the convention, leaders deliberated over how $9 million in yearly fund-raising efforts would be spent. At the same meeting, Hadassah members passed several resolutions addressing foreign policy issues such as the Arab-Israeli conflict, the status of Jews in the Soviet Union, and U.S. support for Israel. In addition, they passed resolutions endorsing civil rights legislation in the United States.[1]

Amid the serious work of geopolitics, civil liberties agitation, and philanthropy, Hadassah members also were treated to a fashion show that showcased designs created by the Hadassah-sponsored Alice Seligsberg Fashion Institute in Israel (Figures 4 and 5).[2] Although fashion shows are not usually thought to be political, Hadassah used fashion shows and beauty culture to attract new members, raise funds, and provide women with a sense of glamour and femininity at a time when women's participation in the public world challenged normative values.

An examination of Hadassah in this time period, in fact, suggests that while mainstream American culture emphasized the worlds of homemaking, consumerism, and beauty culture as the primary acceptable realms for women, women could use beauty-focused culture such as fashion shows, shopping trips, and cosmetics sales as platforms for education and political activism and as a recruitment tool to attract women to political work.[3]

While some scholars might look at these fashion shows and beauty campaigns as ways of encouraging women to engage in consumer culture or as events that supported conservative gender ideals that simply equated women with beauty, this chapter [4] argues that Hadassah's use of beauty culture and fashion shows was more complicated. Hadassah appealed to women through the accepted realm of fashion and beauty while at the same time infusing these activities with political and social messages that challenged the dominant discourse on the role of women in society.

From fairly early on, fashion shows were part of Hadassah's fund-raising and recruitment strategy. Jenna Weissman Joselit suggests that this activity first began in the years between the first and second world wars.[5] This makes sense because Jewish immigrants had used fashion as a means of assimilating and integrating into mainstream American life from the nineteenth century onward.[6]

My own research suggests that by the early 1930s, individual Hadassah and junior Hadassah chapters had begun to sponsor a small number of fashion shows in New York, New Jersey, and Los Angeles.[7] The Hadassah-sponsored fashion show, however, did not really develop on a wide scale or national level until after Israel achieved statehood in 1948. At this juncture, the fashion show became a vehicle for raising funds and attracting women to philanthropic and political work and a new poststatehood women's Zionism. These fashion shows of the post–World War II era differed from earlier fashion shows, not just in their increasing frequency, prominence, and attendance, but also in that they showcased Israeli fashions made by students of Hadassah's Fashion Institute in Israel and that they became conduits for political and ideological action in a time period of heightened gender repression.

Hadassah's fashion shows and beauty events shed light on larger issues in women's historiography. Although Hadassah's use of fashion does not necessarily contradict Betty Friedan's argument that many women in postwar America suffered from limited options, boredom, depression, and the overbearing cultural drive to keep women in the private sphere,[8] it does support recent scholarship that portrays women's experience in the postwar era as complex and varied from a cultural and economic standpoint. In addition, Hadassah's merging of beauty culture and the public sphere validates current scholarship that suggests that women found a variety of ways to challenge the national drive to keep women in the home.[9]

Hadassah was not the first women's group to appeal to existing gender norms to further a public political goal. Women's organizations have historically been a space where women used traditional notions of womanhood for nontraditional public purposes. As early as the nineteenth century, women's groups used the idea of women's and mothers' moral superiority as a springboard from which to engage in political movements such as abolition, temperance, and suffrage.[10]

Margaret Finnegan, for instance, shows how suffragists in the early decades of the twentieth century "strove to sell the movement like a modern commodity" by using fashion and consumerism to engage their audience. They produced goods (such as badges and dolls), displays, and performances.[11] Among other tactics like pageants and parades, suffragists used revolutionary forms of dress like the gender-bending "bloomer" to make political statements.[12] Unlike the suffragists, Hadassah fashion shows generally featured mainstream gender-appropriate styles. The designs presented were not political, but the ways in which Hadassah orchestrated the performative experience of fashion shows and beauty consumption carried gendered and political messages.

While women historically have used existing gender norms as tools for such transformative work as suffrage and abolition, they also used notions about beauty and womanhood in subtler ways in their everyday lives that nevertheless allowed them to carve out a larger space in the public sphere. Beverly Gordon has shown how Jewish and non-Jewish women's charity groups drew on domesticity and commercialism to create women-centered fairs for charity causes. "The elaborate decorations and costuming that created the festive atmosphere were all part of women's domain — decoration and dress are so identified with women, in fact, that even today they comprise the major elements of the 'women's pages' of newspapers and magazines."[13] In much the same way, Hadassah relied upon fashion and beauty culture — pursuits safely identified with women — and used them to engage in the mission of the organization that was highly political and involved working in the public sphere.

Figure 4. Suit at Miami Beach 1958 Convention Fashion Show.
*Photos by Hazel Greenwald, courtesy of Hadassah, The Women's Zionist
Organization of America Inc.*

Hadassah's use of mainstream styles mirrored the larger Jewish community's efforts to integrate into a sometimes hostile gentile America. Like Italians and the Irish, Jews in the nineteenth and early twentieth century were not only often depicted as nonwhite ethnics but also bore the burden of a rather strong vein of anti-Semitism that occasionally manifested itself in prominent places such as Father Charles Coughlin's radio broadcasts, carmaker Henry Ford's *Dearborn Independent*, and minister Gerald L. K. Smith's Christian National Party.[14] By the 1950s, however, Jews as a group had transformed from an immigrant outsider community into a segment of mainstream suburban America. With financial help from the GI Bill and a national public embrace of Jews in light of the Holocaust, Jews moved into a middle-class and white category.[15]

Hadassah's fashion shows and beauty consumption campaigns were conduits for Jewish women in particular to connect themselves with a

Figure 5. Coat at Miami Beach 1958 Convention Fashion Show.
Photos by Hazel Greenwald, courtesy of Hadassah, The Women's Zionist
Organization of America Inc.

more affluent public image. By showcasing fashions that were in the style of high-end European and American fashions and using these displays to raise money and awareness for Hadassah's pro-Israel, pro–civil rights, and civil libertarian agenda, Hadassah members created a Jewish women's middle-class, white-American identity that allowed them to become political and social activists. Such efforts prompted and sometimes required women to be participants in the political arena at a time when gender prescriptions dictated that they remain at home and tend to their families.

Scholars like Lois Banner argue that while fashion and beauty have at times provided women positive sites for escapist fantasy and pleasure, "of all of the elements of women's separate culture, the pursuit of beauty has been the most divisive and ultimately the most oppressive."[16] The 1950s, Banner argues, brought with it a reinstatement of Victorian ideals of beauty, emphasizing the binding of women's bodies through the corset and hoop skirts that resembled Victorian fashions and gender sensibilities. Fashions and beauty ideals often have shaped the ways in which women express and understand gender roles.

Other historians have emphasized the liberating aspects of fashion and beauty culture. Kathy Peiss and Nan Enstad, for instance, argue that fashion and consumerism provided the immigrant working-class Jewish women of New York's garment district around the turn of the century a voice and a language for a new Americanized and, in some ways, liberated class and gender consciousness.[17] Through Hadassah fashion shows and beauty culture, we see that both of these arguments are valid. While beauty culture and fashion have the potential to objectify women, lower their self-esteem, and minimize their intellectual abilities,[18] there can be situations, as is the case with Hadassah, where fashion and beauty serve as a vehicle for empowerment.[19]

For Hadassah, fashion shows were often rooted in a complex give-and-take regarding women's roles. Hadassah fashion shows, in fact, highlighted the duality that marked the organization's attempts to wrestle with the role women should play in society. On the one hand, Hadassah encouraged its members to be educated political leaders, activists, and lobbyists. On the other hand, Hadassah focused on women's roles as mothers through an appeal to maternalism. In addition, Hadassah appealed to women's role as beauty culture consumers to attract new members and celebrate Hadassah achievements.

FASHION SHOWS

It was not unusual for women's organizations to sponsor fashion shows during the post–World War II era. In fact, Alexandra Palmer finds that many different types of women's organizations worked with department stores to stage fund-raising fashion shows featuring models wearing department store couture.[20] What was unique about Hadassah's shows is that they displayed fashions created by female students at Hadassah's own Fashion Institute in Israel. The fashion shows also often included an educational or political component.

Figure 6

Photo by Hazel Greenwald, courtesy of Hadassah,
The Women's Zionist Organization of America Inc.

Established as showcases for Hadassah's educational design programs in Israel, the fashion shows also provided Israeli women an opportunity to gain career training and to begin to make an entré into the male-dominated international fashion industry. In establishing fashion shows that displayed students' designs, Hadassah leaders of the 1950s and 1960s were drawing from widely published comments Henrietta Szold had made in 1941 about the necessity of vocational training for women and girls in Israel. Szold had argued that the training of women in gender-appropriate careers would lead to national development: "The girl in Palestine has no opportunity to learn a trade or profession. There isn't a good dressmaker, there isn't a good secretary, there is no good cook, and the reasons—there is no school."[21]

Figure 7.

Photo courtesy of Hadassah, The Women's Zionist Organization of America Inc.

Four and a half years after Szold's death on November 3, 1949, Hadassah members responded to Szold's charge by opening a Fashion Institute at Hadassah's Alice Seligsberg Vocational Trade School for Girls in Jerusalem and admitting 26 female students.[22] The mission of the Fashion Institute was to train girls in fashion design and then to use their talents and knowledge to rival European dominance in the fashion industry. "The goal is to produce a 'flying wedge of experts'... who after

Figure 8.

Photo courtesy of Hadassah, The Women's Zionist Organization of America Inc.

two years of study of original fashion design and pattern making will open salons and take key positions in mass production dress factories now springing up in Israel."[23]

A month later, at the thirty-fifth annual Hadassah convention in the United States, Hadassah launched its first Israel-focused fashion show, showcasing designs produced by professionals in the Israeli apparel industry. The work of Fashion Institute students was displayed in subsequent years and became a regular feature of the show.[24]

At the 1949 event, which Hadassah officials labeled the "first fashion show of Israel couture," American models exhibited 15 fashions. According to publicity materials and organizational records related to the event, Hadassah's American membership seemed captivated. "The 'eternal feminine' angel," one member explained, "was sharply evident during the fashion show."[25] The designs ranged from "cocktail lounge attire" to a "dance frock" to "knitted suits" and "evening glamour." Exotic "oriental" influences of the Middle East were noted to be a trademark of the designs, which were promoted as having "unique Israel influences."[26] Clothing with intricate "embroideries are done painstakingly by hand by Jews from Yemen, who use motifs handed down for generations," according to Hadassah records of the event.[27] In addition, the influences of French and American fashions also were emphasized: this clothing, although designed in Israel, bridged East and West, according to show organizers.[28] Hadassah leaders such as Dr. Miriam Freund, vocational education chair, participated as models, attending the conference wearing a Western-style three-piece suit that had been displayed in the fashion show (Figure 6).[29]

After the success of the first fashion show, a second show in 1950, featuring the designs of the Seligsberg Fashion Institute students, went on the road throughout the United States. Throughout the 1950s and 1960s new designs and themes were presented each year at national Hadassah conferences. In addition to the Israel fashion shows, some Hadassah chapters continued to run fashion shows sponsored by local industry.[30] Hadassah women were particularly innovative in publicizing, promoting, and organizing the annual convention events, traveling fashion shows, and local revues. Members attending the 1950 traveling show could purchase a narrative script to read along with the designs as the models walked down the runway. There was such demand that garments had to be air-expressed or hand delivered from show to show.[31] At later shows, individual members also could purchase a "fashion fan," a 4-inch by 4-inch hand-held fan with a series of watercolor sketches of the fashions from the shows. Chapter leaders too could purchase a "packaged store window display" for publicity purposes that included a photo mount of the fashions in the show and mountings of the designs on wire frames.[32]

By January 1950, only two months after the second convention showcase, twenty chapters, from Milwaukee and Peoria to Beverly Hills, had booked appearances of the traveling show.[33] Ultimately, the fashion show became a successful tool for fund-raising and attracting members. In some cases, especially active members were honored at the show or rewarded with spots as models. In Birmingham, Alabama, only "active chapter chairmen or workers" received the honor of modeling the clothes.[34] As they walked down the runway, their names and positions in Hadassah were announced, creating a situation in which the performative act of everyday women engaging in beauty culture and glamour via fashion shows was coupled with Hadassah's political and philanthropic goals.[4]

By honoring Hadassah leadership through the fashion shows, Hadassah found a way to use traditional gender roles to recognize women for participating in the public sphere. Hadassah leaders often worked very long hours and saw their work in the organization as a full-time job. In addition, as discussed in chapter four, Hadassah literature coached women on how to manage their husbands' objections to their time spent out of the home and at Hadassah events.[36]

During a period when important segments of popular culture and society objected to women in the workplace and in the public sphere, Hadassah was able to weave into the fashion shows a reminder of the validity of women's work and engagement in political and philanthropic activism.[37] Showcased before 400 attendees, the climactic final act of the Birmingham show in 1952 was a model walking the runway modeling a very unglamorous item of dress, a nurse's uniform. This nurse's uniform, the symbol of Hadassah's medical program in Israel and the actual uniform worn by many Hadassah workers there, was thus transfigured into a gown of beauty. This transformation glamorized both the work of nurses and the participation of Hadassah members as their political and philanthropic supporters—both areas in which women engaged in public work.[38]

The third Hadassah convention fashion show, in 1951, featured twelve designs with names that reflected their design inspiration. The

Mimosa, for example, was a wool coat featuring wide hip pockets and exaggerated collar (Figure 7).[39] An example of eveningwear was the Nightingale, a gunmetal strapless taffeta dress with black velvet stripes and borders. Black jade lined the bodice (Figure 8). Some designs also continued to feature Middle-Eastern-inspired Israeli- or Yemenite-style apparel.

Local chapters often took elaborate steps to promote their fashion shows. In Detroit, Michigan, the theater for the fashion show had been decorated to resemble an Israeli airport; 2,500 people attended the show. The fantasy was complete with usherettes donning the stewardess outfits of EL-AL, the national Israeli airline, and a ramp emerging from a replica plane door. Models wearing EL-AL-inspired fashions then emerged from a "Plane from Israel."[40] The fashion shows lauded the work of women outside the home as fashion designers, flight attendants, and Hadassah activists. Because many EL-AL stewardesses received training at the Hadassah Hotel Management School in Israel, the fashion shows also acknowledged the work done by Hadassah in Israel. Thus, the EL-AL show combined fund-raising with support for women's education, for working women, and for a growing political campaign to purchase Israeli-made goods and services — all the while promoting an acceptable American focus on women's beauty.[41]

Ultimately celebrity began to appear at the Hadassah fashion shows, adding a level of glamour to the Israeli students' designs. At the 1954 national convention, prominent television personalities lent their names to the fashion show segment: "Dressed in the latest creation of Seligsberg School girls — A Hadassah school in Israel of fashion design — an Israel model descends from an EL-AL plane and is welcomed by Tex McCrary and his wife, Jinx, stars of the 'Tex and Jinx' television show."[42] Jinx Falkenburg, a well-known model and actress, and her husband McCrary, had a celebrity interview television show that was extremely popular among the viewing audience.[43] Hadassah members and their children modeled clothes at this event.[44]

EAST MEETS WEST

Fashion had the power not only to make women feel beautiful but also to take them to different parts of the world. Designs that featured veils, harem pants, tunic tops, and Middle Eastern motifs expressed the complexity of Jewish ethnic identity in Israel and in the United States (Figure 9). This interplay could be read as objectifying Middle Eastern Jewish and non-Jewish women, including Yemenite and Asian Indian Jews as well as Arabs, by playing into stereotypes that were exotic. While the actual Jewish population of Israel originated from both Europe and the Middle East, Jews of European descent, or *Ashkenazim*, comprised the largest portion of the population throughout the 1950s and into the 1960s. This began to change as massive waves of immigration brought *Mizrachim*, or "Eastern" Jews, from countries such as Yemen, Morocco, Iraq, Persia, India, and Turkey. By the late 1960s, the population of Israel had shifted from an Ashkenazi majority to a majority of Jews hailing from Muslim countries.[45]

Nevertheless, the "exotic" Middle-Eastern-style fashions modeled during the 1950s- and 1960s-era shows connected Israel and Israelis with the traditions of the Middle East and southern Asia in the minds of American Jewish women and created a sense of place and permanency for supporters and residents of the new Jewish state, especially in the early years of nationhood. Ethnic design elements also allowed American Jews to distance themselves from Israel by setting up Middle Easterners, *Mizrachim*, Indians, and even European-origin Israelis as exotic.[46]

Publicity about the Fashion Institute in the early 1950s stressed the "East meets West" elements of student designers' style: "These young people of Israel who have turned to fashion design are cleverly utilizing the elements of exotic color, texture, and fabric which surround them in their Middle Eastern environment. It is not surprising that some of their most successful and original designs incorporated the graceful sumptuousness of eastern dress into the practical garb of the West."[47]

One can see the emphasis on the merging of East and West by

examining photographs of the designs from the era. At the 1950 San Francisco convention, for example, a model displayed a two-piece "cocktail frock" in brown taffeta. The full-length outfit, complete with gold embroidery, which Hadassah promoters described as "tunic-style," had perhaps just a hint of Middle-eastern style influence (Figure 9).[48]

A second design from the same convention, however, demonstrated a much stronger attempt to capture Middle-eastern influences. Also a tunic-style dress, it featured elaborate gold embroidery layered over a narrow black skirt (Figure 10).[49] Fashions showcased at the 1952–1953 convention in Detroit went a step further in emphasizing perceptions about the folk forms of dress in the East and Middle East, while still giving a salutary nod to developments in Western European dress (Figure 11).[50] On the left hand we see a woman modeling fashions reportedly based on a traditional gown and headpiece worn by Jewish women immigrating to Israel from India. In the center stands a model wearing a modern Israeli gown in white ribbed pique with black embroidery. And on the right is a gown that borrows from traditional Yemenite Jewish dress.[51]

By wearing clothes designed by Israeli women and sponsoring their careers, Hadassah members sought to uplift Israeli women, while also creating a bridge between the women of the two countries. But Hadassah publications also emphasized the differences, using stereotypes and notions about Israeli women to either reinforce or challenge traditional gender roles for Jewish American women. Hadassah columnist Molly Lyons Bar-David, author of the

Figure 9.

Photo courtesy of Hadassah, The Women's Zionist Organization of America Inc.

Hadassah Newsletter column "Diary of a Jerusalem Housewife," wrote *Women in Israel*, a book circulated and published by Hadassah in 1952. In it, Bar-David reflected on some of the issues involved in American Jewish representations of Israeli women. According to Bar-David, women in Israel were not known for their beauty or glamour, but were more concerned with working the land than with personal appearance. The pioneer woman "has deliberately turned her back on comfort and ease" in pursuit of higher ideals and the struggle for nationhood, an effort that "leaves marks of experience and wear... The b o d y beautiful is little cultivated and the glamour girl not greatly glorified in Israel. This may in part be because of the fact that the stimulus — competition — is lacking, for there are more men than enough to go around."[52]

But what women in Israel lacked in beauty, Bar-David argued, they made up for in persistence and brainpower: "In perhaps no other country do women play such an important role among their people as the women in Israel. In every sphere women of intelligence and ability have proved themselves equal to men in laying the foundations of the new state."[53] While suggesting that Israeli women could serve as a model for independent American women, her insistence that the lack of men and the nontraditional roles Israeli women had begun to play in society had led to a deficiency of beauty, fashion sense, and femininity, also pointed to the feared downside of feminism and women's emancipation: the threat that women might lose their gender identity.

Discussions of women in Israel brought to the

Figure 10.

Photo courtesy of Hadassah, The Women's Zionist
Organization of America Inc.

surface anxiety over the roles of Jewish women in American society. What did they want to learn, and what did they want to reject from their Israeli sisters? These questions carried a complex set of answers that often provided contradictory messages about American and Israeli womanhood. Through fashion shows and participation in beauty culture Hadassah members distinguished themselves from Israeli women and confirmed that even politically active American Jewish women would adhere to socially acceptable beauty and gender norms.

While fashion shows helped Hadassah link beauty culture with the organization's political and philanthropic aims, emphasis on women's appearance and women's roles as consumers began to inundate more and more facets of Hadassah's fund-raising and political efforts throughout the 1950s and 1960s. Hadassah women, and Jewish women in general, were invited by the organization to participate in shopping sprees, sewing circles, consumption of beauty products, and fund-raisers focused on beauty in images of working women (such as flight attendants and nurses). Thus, Hadassah members continued to use beauty culture as a means to further the organization's political agenda in the domestic and international sphere.

In doing so, Hadassah stressed a unique brand of consumerism that wed beauty products and traditional consumption practices with political and organizational goals. Consumer culture in the 1950s and 1960s served as both a status symbol for the emergent suburban middle-class and simultaneously as a definer of gender roles for women and men. The national emphasis in the postwar era glorified the middle-class housewife and prescribed shopping and house maintenance as among her most essential duties. As Elaine Tyler May argues, women's consumerism and appearance played an important role in the national Cold War image of American womanhood by juxtaposing the beauty and domestic expertise of American women against the allegedly inferior Soviet women. Jewish women also participated in this rise of women's consumer culture.[54]

Hadassah members once again borrowed from dominant notions about the gender roles of the day and utilized them for purposes that often challenged the hegemonic focus on the home. One of Hadassah's strategies was to channel women's consumerism into fund-raising

Figure 11.
Photo courtesy of Hadassah, The Women's Zionist Organization of America Inc.

efforts. Examples of this are numerous in Hadassah's activities in the 1950s. In March 1952, at a Hadassah membership conference in New York City, 500 women gathered for a "shopping expedition":

> At about 1:10 pm the staring became more intense as a few smartly bedecked women carrying brown shopping bags paraded through the lobby.... By 1:30 the lobby habitués of the Park Sheraton were caught up in a mass invasion of shopping bags. Scores upon scores of women were carrying them ballroom bound.[55]

The shopping bags carried a logo that explained that Hadassah members were going shopping for "ways and means of bringing 40,000 new members into Hadassah" in honor of Hadassah's fortieth anniversary.[56]

In addition to consuming fashion and going shopping, some Hadassah members also formed sewing circles, a seemingly conventional form of women's culture that was nevertheless involved in a political and nation-building goal of producing clothes to send to Israel. Cutters from the International Ladies Garment Workers Union (ILGWU), an American trade union with a high Jewish membership that was particularly strong in New York, were enlisted as volunteers on occasion to assist in the production of large quantities of clothing to be sent to Hadassah's philanthropic operations in Israel. That many ILGWU workers were themselves Jewish helped assist Hadassah in enlisting union members in the effort. By forming relationship with unions such as the garment workers, Hadassah, a largely middle- to upper-middle-class organization, brought in working-class volunteers.[57]

On a local level, individual chapters of Hadassah found innovative ways to fund-raise, educate, and advocate Zionism that also involved fashion and beauty consumption. Focusing on accepted female interests such as self-beautification, many chapters held "days of beauty" programs where Hadassah members raised money and awareness for their political causes. In much the same way that fashion shows provided an avenue for women to engage in political and social activism while partaking in a normative feminine activity, so too other activities associated with femininity and women's sphere provided outlets for participation. The Yonkers chapter organized a "day for beauty" for its members at which they received manicures and facials in return for donations. "Usually 100 ladies gathered together for lunch is food for gossip," reported the local Hadassah newsletter. However, in this case "it resulted in a tidy sum for Youth Aliyah, a youth rescue mission."[58]

Some members in Westchester's Sabra chapter offered services as baby sitters, typists, caterers, hairdressers, seamstresses, and chauffeurs in order to raise funds.[59] Thus, women who did not tend to work outside the home used their skills and worked toward fund-raising. Members could enjoy a traditionally feminine occupation, a day at a beauty salon.

Or they could extend themselves into a workplace-like environment at club headquarters in order to fund-raise. One successful fund-raiser involved holding movie preview nights at local theaters with dinner afterward.[60] Other popular fund-raising activities included rummage sales and the managing of local Hadassah thrift stores, in addition to benefit luncheons and dinners.[61]

Unlike the Hadassah of the 1950s, which had championed Hadassah activities as the proper extension of Jewish women's role, the Hadassah of the 1960s empowered women to widen the acceptable role of middle-class and upper-class housewives. While Hadassah participation remained a vital avenue for women's expression and voice, Hadassah leaders, magazines, and resolutions encouraged the organization's membership to accept a variety of women's roles including working outside the home, and becoming educated and publicly engaged. At the same time, however, Hadassah incorporated an even stronger emphasis on fashion, beauty, and glamour.

Already in full swing in the 1950s, Hadassah fashion shows continued to remain a part of Hadassah life through the 1960s. Every annual Hadassah convention since its inception had showcased political leaders and such sessions typically dealt with subjects such as religion, politics, and social welfare. Alongside these crucial topics, Hadassah conventions also continued to include fashion shows of apparel made in Israel at Hadassah's Alice Seligsberg Vocational School. A Hadassah member joked about the odd pairing: "Only Hadassah women, it should be noted, can attend to serious business and sigh with delight at beautiful clothes — and even quote the Talmud for approval on both."[62]

FASHION, HADASSAH, AND THE 1960S

Hadassah publications of the 1960s featured descriptions of women in the professions, and presented in-depth analyses of women in positions of power — from doctors to legislators. In addition, they also positively represented women, both in Israel and America, who were working in traditionally female occupations such as secretaries, teachers, and nurses. In the 1950s, working women were depicted as single, but the 1960s Hadassah articles provided a roadmap for Jewish women who wanted both to work and raise a family. Articles like "Secretary and Homemaker," published in *Hadassah Magazine* in 1964 described a day in the life of an Israeli homemaker who also worked as a secretary. The balance between career and motherhood, although portrayed as difficult, also was shown as rewarding and commonplace. In the 1950s, Hadassah articles and literature presented Israeli women workers as strange or completely different from American Jewish women, but the 1964 article presented work outside the home as a part of a normal life and argued in a positive manner that women in Israel and America both worked and raised families in order to make ends meet.[63]

While Hadassah challenged the role of women in the private sphere by advocating women's political participation and by representing women as having life choices that included work and education, the organization continued to appeal to American "housewives." As one chapter president put it, Jewish history and the variety of programs offered by Hadassah explained why "318,000 American housewives in 49 of our beloved United States have been magnetized by our democratic history-making and humanitarian endeavors."[64]

By the early 1960s, Hadassah circulated an annual "Master Kit" to all members. The kit included the most current educational information, brochures, advertisements, programming guides, and fund-raising tools. The kit thus provided Hadassah members with an overview of the various activities and programs available to them. The 1960–61 edition of the kit was conceived partly as a marketing tool based on the advertising philosophy of the fashion industry. An interview in *Hadassah Magazine* with Mina Brownstone, Hadassah promotion director, explained that she borrowed from high-fashion stylists in order to create her new "line" of promotional materials, modeled after "Paris High Style." Knowing that women paid attention to the "fashion practices and modes which make up their lives in America," Hadassah literature must, she argued, "compete with all the slick, gay, 'image building' mail our women receive from others who have something to sell, even though *we* are selling an idea and an ideal."[65] Thus, to "sell the ideal" of Hadassah throughout the 1960s, Hadassah incorporated concepts from the fashion and beauty world to attract members and to sustain interest. In addition, the heightened use of fashion and beauty culture was coupled with a stronger push for women's political action at home through new Hadassah poverty programs aligned with Lyndon Johnson's Great Society, resolutions expressing concern with nuclear proliferation, continued support of the United Nations through a Hadassah liaison, and lobbying efforts on behalf of Israel amid events like the 1967 War.

One way Hadassah further incorporated beauty culture was by selling Hadassah boxed lipsticks to raise money. The lipsticks bore the imprint "Put Hadassah on Every Women's Lips." They could be purchased in sets of 100, although only one shade was offered.[66] Another "member getting gimmick" included boxing membership information in an attractive "plastic coin purse."[67] Mrs. Morris Kertzer, chair of the national supplies committee, suggested that Hadassah utilize women's interest in fashion for fund raising activities.[68] She argued that since new fashion trends included shorter hem lines, chapters should go into the business of shortening hems: "set up shop for a talented volunteer seamstress, charge the going rate per hem and let over-the-knee put you over-the-top in supplies" for member activities.[69]

If members could not gain access to the fashion show in person they could purchase a series of slides of the fashion shows to screen to Hadassah members with accompanying texts as a way to raise funds for Hadassah vocational programs. A 1962 virtual fashion show, entitled "What is a Dress," contained eighty-eight slides of dresses designed by Seligsberg students, with "clearly written script" accompanying the slides. A unique feature of the show was "a series of introductory cartoons which cleverly depict the meaning of a dress to a woman, to her husband, and others."[70] A movement to buy Israeli fashions in America also gained ground during the 1960s.[71]

An examination of Hadassah's use of fashion and beauty culture in the post–World War II era points to the fact that fashion and beauty culture can and did have explicit political and empowering uses. At the same time, however, this phenomenon was a complex negotiation between the empowering aspects of the use of fashion and beauty consumption and the restrictive implications of such gender tropes.

Hadassah successfully appealed to women's public action through gender appropriate forms of expression like fashion and beauty culture. Hadassah conveyed messages about womanhood, politics, and Jewish identity to Hadassah members and by extension to their families.

CHAPTER VI

FROM THE SIX-DAY WAR TO NUCLEAR DISARMAMENT: HADASSAH AND FOREIGN POLICY IN THE 1960S

In 1968, as outgoing president of Hadassah, Charlotte Jacobson addressed more than 2,000 Hadassah delegates at the national convention in Chicago. She issued a plea to Arab nations to negotiate for peace. The only way to end tensions in the Middle East, she argued, was through peace talks. Nasser and Arab leaders refused to engage in productive discussions, she said. Jacobson appealed to her audience by noting that Hadassah was an organization that "holds out its hand of friendship to all the Arab people, inviting them to share in the medical knowledge and facilities of our great medical center."[1] Her statements reflected the complex position of Hadassah foreign policy and views of Arabs during the 1960s.

As American Cold War ideology continued to stress the importance of maintaining a balance of power in the world through both diplomatic and military efforts, Hadassah also engaged in Cold War rhetoric to secure the position of Israel in the Middle East. Hadassah members learned about the Arab-Israel conflict in the 1960s through Hadassah literature, resolutions, meetings, and seminars. As the sixties progressed and public opinion turned a critical eye toward Israeli policies and stances vis-à-vis the Arab world and the Palestinians, Hadassah armed its members with data and talking points about "Arab propaganda," while at the same time assuring Arabs from Israel and elsewhere full access to their medical center and some social programs in Israel.

During the 1960s, Hadassah labored to ensure that Israel continued to receive foreign aid from the United States. To that end, Hadassah consistently lobbied government officials on the importance Israel played strategically in a Middle East divided by Cold War interests. With the Soviets backing countries such as Syria and Egypt, Israel — a democratic country and ally of the United States — served, according to Hadassah, as a fortress of democratic values in a sea of Soviet-backed Arab aggression. Essential to that argument, Hadassah stressed the vulnerability of Israel to Arab attacks, both economic and military in nature. On the economic front, Hadassah argued that Israel had to contend with economically hostile Arab countries that worked to deny Israel access to important environmental resources such as water, while they boycotted Israeli products. On the military front, the Soviets, Hadassah explained, had armed the Arab nations with an arsenal of effective weaponry, while Israel struggled to maintain a defensive army. Hadassah communicated through a variety of mediums, both to its members and to the outside world, that Arab nations sought to destroy Israel and that Israel sought only peaceful coexistence.

Beginning in 1960, Hadassah started to assert the danger of an "arms imbalance" in the Middle East and urged the U.S. government to provide economic assistance to Israel. Hadassah worked to guarantee that the United States not "tolerate discrimination against Arab firms who do business with Israel." [2] At the Pittsburgh National Convention in 1962, Hadassah adopted a new resolution designed to put pressure on the U.S. government to encourage talks between Israel and Arab governments. The resolution warned of the growing threat Egypt posed to Israel and to world security more generally. The United States should, "take such steps as are necessary to remedy the dangerous arms imbalance resulting from Egypt's possession of the most modern military material."[3] Resolutions adopted at Hadassah conventions throughout the 1960s argued that the United States should continue to support Israel through foreign aid.[4]

Similarly, Hadassah endorsed legislation designed to curtail the use of American foreign aid for military buildup of nations aggressive to the United States or its allies.[5] A resolution adopted at the Hadassah national convention of 1964 urged the United States to maintain foreign aid programs as an arm of its foreign policy and a weapon in the struggle against poverty and economic problems in the world and as a means to secure "peaceful cooperation with other nations."[6] The resolution acknowledged the benefits that economic aid had bestowed upon Israel in a "peaceful economic aid endeavor" and urged that funds not be utilized to promote war.[7]

Hadassah successfully endorsed the message that Israel should receive foreign aid, but that hostile Arab nations should not. At the February 1965 Mid-Winter Conference, Hadassah adopted a resolution arguing that American foreign aid should be given only to countries intent upon using funds for "peaceful economic development, and not as a means to release funds for building military establishments designed for aggression against allies of the United States, or to subvert United States objectives in any way."[8] The resolution further made clear that the president of the United States should assure that countries, like the United Arab Republic, receiving funding from the United States not be allowed to engage in such activities.[9]

By the 1966 annual convention held in Boston, Massachusetts, Hadassah thanked Congress in a resolution for expressing "its opposition to giving economic assistance to the United Arab Republic, so long as it continues to acquire vast supplies of sophisticated Soviet weapons, threatening the security of Israel and its neighbors."[10] Other resolutions adopted at the midwinter and annual conference in 1965 stressed the importance of U.S. support of Israel in a hostile region, led by Nasser and the nations of the Arab League that desired the destruction of Israel.[11] Hadassah's resolutions expressed the threat of Arab aggression in the Middle East as directly tied to Cold War dynamics: "Hadassah notes with growing concern the continuing flow of conventional and sophisticated arms from the U.S.S.R. to Egypt, and the continuing insistence of Egypt's president that war with Israel was inevitable."[12] By the 1966 convention, Hadassah in a resolution thanked President Johnson for allowing Israel to "acquire deterrent weapons in the United States" and to support Israel through diplomacy.[13]

Other resolutions adopted at conventions in 1965 and 1966 urged the United States to continue to support Israel through foreign aid. In addition, the resolutions stipulated that countries receiving foreign aid from the United States not be allowed to "engage in economic warfare"[14] against countries also receiving support. In later resolutions, Hadassah continued to urge the U.S. government to challenge the Arab boycott and to ensure that U.S. businesspeople did not succumb to Arab pressure.[15]

A Seven Point Middle East program, crafted by Hadassah leadership, served throughout the 1960s as its cornerstone for foreign policy issues in the Middle East. Point one urged the United States to "oppose aggression in the Middle East."[16] The second point stated that the U.S. administration should "take effective measures to insure that an arms imbalance shall not result in the Middle East."[17] Points three and five emphasized that the United States not support any Arab countries refusing to do business with Israelis firms or "wage economic warfare" against other countries also receiving assistance from the United States. Point four urged the administration to secure the Suez Canal as an open waterway for all countries, including Israel, while point six offered a controversial remedy to the situation of Arab refugees in Israel, arguing that they should be resettled in Arab countries. (The issue of Arab refugees will be discussed more fully later in the chapter.) Point seven remained a central tenant of Hadassah throughout the 1960s, that the United States should promote "direct negotiations between Israel and the Arab States."[18] Israeli leadership echoed this sentiment promoted by Hadassah in its various publications and pamphlets in the 1960s. The fact that Arabs refused to negotiate with Israel was seen as the roadblock to peace.[19]

Another factor that shifted Hadassah dynamics was the emergence of a new relationship between Hadassah and the American Israel Public Affairs Committee (AIPAC) in the 1960s. Founded in 1954 as a pro-Israel lobby, AIPAC would become an extremely influential political action lobbying group. With only 65,000 members today, AIPAC wields enormous power in Washington, DC. Although not well known even within most of the Jewish community until the 1980s, Hadassah paid attention to AIPAC policies early on.[20] In the 1960s, the Hadassah Zionist Affairs Committee included a copy of the *Near East Report*, a publication of AIPAC that addressed Middle East politics, in Hadassah Kits. Hadassah leaders described AIPAC as an "authoritative" interpreter of events in the Middle East to the American public and government officials. In addition to circulating AIPAC's *Near East Report* and resolutions to Hadassah members, the chairperson of the Zionist Affairs Committee attended AIPAC's annual conference.[21] Hadassah Zionist Affairs also circulated copies of AIPAC's conference resolutions.

Members were urged to study the document carefully and to circulate it widely among their members.[22] AIPAC materials consistently warned of the threat the Arab world posed to Israel. Like Hadassah, AIPAC viewed the tensions among Israel, Palestinians, and neighboring countries, through a Cold War lens.[23]

A central tenant of Hadassah's mission was to lobby the U.S. government to continue financial and military backing of Israel by the United States through foreign aid and weapons deals. Hadassah sought to accomplish this by educating its members and their families and by lobbying government officials on this issue. The Cold War context provided an avenue for Hadassah to argue that support of Israel worked to ensure a balance of power in the Middle East. The fact that hostile Arab nations surrounded Israel's borders also provided a strong argument for the necessity of backing Israel and monitoring financial aid to Arab countries.

In an article published in *Hadassah Magazine*, Hadassah members learned of the complications affecting the sale of Phantom supersonic jet bombers to Israel. Members learned of the positive impact of weapons sales to the survival of Israel and the balance of power in the Middle East. "Israel must play a critical role in resisting the consequences of the Soviet build up. Therefore Israel's possession of the phantoms is not only important to her but to the United States as well." The article further decried the fact that "lengthy political negotiations" had slowed the process of Israel's acquisition of weapons.[24] The Pentagon's desire to avoid an escalation of the conflict in the Middle East had resulted in it asking Israel to ratify the "treaty banning the spread of atomic weapons."[25] The article suggested that Israel should have full access to U.S. weapons and that no "strings" should be attached. Ironically, while Hadassah fully supported Israel on any stances it took regarding nuclear weapons treaties, it urged the United States to ratify the treaty. [26]

THE SIX-DAY WAR

The Six-Day War of 1967 created major political shock waves and shifted perceptions about Israel and Zionism. Responding to the ominous prewar atmosphere in the Middle East, Hadassah ran ads in *Hadassah Headlines*, aimed at raising money for Israel in the event of a war. The advertisements urged Hadassah leaders to call emergency board meetings in their local communities and to "push hard for more members and plus-dollars."[27] On the morning of June 5, when the fighting officially began, Hadassah headquarters in New York served as a makeshift central command for Hadassah's efforts to support the war. Hospitals and drug companies donated over a half million dollars' worth of medications. Volunteer pharmacists and Hadassah volunteers sifted through the donations and packaged them for shipping to Israel. In addition, donations of other types of medical devices, such a prosthetics, syringes, and even beds, had to be routed to Hadassah hospital in Israel. Hadassah representatives contacted Rabbi Emanuel Rackman of Yeshiva University for permission to work on the holiday of Shavuot in order to get supplies out rapidly. The rabbi responded that saving lives came first and that the prohibition of not working on the holiday could be overlooked for that purpose.[28]

After six days of war, Israel triumphantly emerged as the dominant military force in the Middle East. Israel had decimated the Jordanian air force, significantly weakened the world's image of Egypt's military capabilities, and made their point to Syria that state-backed terrorism was not to be tolerated. The Six-Day War not only proved Israel's military superiority but also significantly changed the borders within the Fertile Crescent. Israel later annexed Syria's Golan Heights, a strategic mountain range on the border of Israel and Syria that had been the source of many of the Fatah incursions. In addition, Israel took possession of the Sinai Peninsula of Egypt — which they traded in 1979 for a peace agreement with Egypt. Lastly, but most significantly, Israel captured the West Bank of Jordan, which included the old city of Jerusalem, the center of the Jewish, Muslim, and Christian faiths. For Jews, the old city housed one of the most holy sites — the remnants

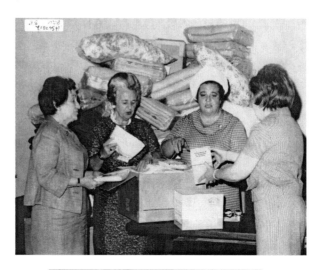

Figure 12. Packing emergency supplies for Israel at Hadassah's national office, 1967. Left to right: Hannah Goldberg, Bea Usdan, Gladys Zales, Charlotte Jacobson

Photo courtesy of Hadassah, The Women's Zionist Organization of America Inc.

of the great temple that had been destroyed by the Romans in 70 CE. The outer wall, called the Western Wall, is said to be the holiest space in Judaism, where one can feel the presence of G-d. Along with the wall also came many other Jewish historical sites. Although the West Bank had been part of Jordan, it housed a large Palestinian population. Thus began one of the most controversial aspects of Israeli history. Historians with differing political perspectives disagree strongly on the correct historical narrative.

Edith Zamost, a member of the Hadassah National Board in 1967, reflected on Hadassah activism. As she tried to enter Hadassah House on Fifty-second Street: "I found I could not go beyond the front door. The lobby was piled high with supplies contributed for our medical center in Jerusalem. I was directed to the meeting room at the nearby bank and in that ordinary room, I saw arrayed before me the extraordinary leaders of Hadassah."[29]

Hadassah Magazine published a special edition on the Six-Day War. Renowned author and Holocaust survivor Elie Wiesel wrote an essay about the significance of capturing the Western Wall:

They tell me this is the Wall. No. I don't believe it... This is the first time I am here, yet I feel that I was at this very spot before. I have already seen these Jews, have heard their prayers. Every shape seems familiar, every sound as if it has arisen from the depths of my own past. But there is a difference. Before there were no young men and women milling about in uniforms. [30]

Wiesel reflected upon the unique vantage point of these soldiers as both warriors and Jews witnessing a historical moment. "Indeed," he contended, "the coverage of this war should be handled not only by newspaper columnists and military experts but by poets and Kabbalists as well, 'for, what has happened cannot be described in neat, logical terms.'"[31] For many years, the Western Wall had been in the hands of the Jordanians, and Israelis had been denied entry into Jordan and the wall. Wiesel urged Hadassah readers to secure the wall within Jewish hands: "The events that took place have finally freed Israel from the paralyzing chains of 'logic.' Let the world know: Two plus two equals two thousand years when the subject is the wall and its stones. Even the almighty cannot allow what has happened to become as though it had not happened."[32]

In July 1967, Hadassah's Zionist Affairs Committee circulated a kit for use as the basis for special sessions designed to educate Hadassah youth and adults about Israeli history, the Arab-Israeli conflict, and the importance of a united Jerusalem.[33] The kit also included a copy of AIPAC's July issue of the *Near East Report*. It criticized U.S. ties with Jordan and argued for more U.S. aid to Israel.[34]

In a "Basic Information Kit" distributed by Hadassah in July 1967, the Zionist Affairs Committee included a section entitled "Israel — Never an Arab Land." In this section, Hadassah offered a historical interpretation that argued that Arabs had manufactured a "myth" that "Israel and the whole of mandatory Palestine, was stolen from the Arabs as a result of imperialist machinations and settled by alien Jews."[35] Responding to a growing international critique of Israel as aligned with imperialism and expansionism, Hadassah spent much of the aftermath of the 1967 War in a defensive posture — explaining that Israel had a historical, political, and spiritual right to exist and to defend itself. Arabs had not maintained a historic prerogative to the area, according to Hadassah, because an Arab land of Palestine never existed in Israel. Rather:

the one people that has in fact maintained its historic and religious connection with the area called Palestine, over a period of 2000 years, is the Jews. Their right to the land is not only based on history and sentiment but is claimed by the physical process of the work invested in transforming it into an area capable of supporting life. It is the fruits of this work that motivate mythological Arab claims to the territory.[36]

Throughout the 1960s, Hadassah's portrayals of Arabs and Arab states grew more critical. Depictions of Arabs as lackeys of the USSR and hostile toward Israel dominated Hadassah's coverage of events in the Middle East. One example of this type of coverage occurred when Hadassah reported on the Eichmann trial taking place in Israel:

The Arab countries are bitterly opposed to Eichmann being tried in Israel. They know full well that they will be implicated in the Nazi genocide crimes by Eichman's testimony. "Captured photographs now available as documentary evidence in Israel show the Mufti of Jerusalem with Eichmann, standing at the Auschwitz railroad siding watching a transport of Jews being unloaded from a stinking cattle train and herded toward the gas chambers." It was the Mufti that urged Hitler to exterminate all Jews if he wanted the support of Arab nationalists.[37]

Arab propaganda was something about which Hadassah literature and seminars educated the organization's members about:

To turn to the ever present problem of the Middle East, the USSR and Egypt have issued a new propaganda offensive, with the object of conditioning public opinion to view that Egypt is ready to make concessions, and that Israel is immovable. We must be cautious against being influenced by Soviet and Arab efforts to appear flexible and peaceful. Nasser spelled out the real Egyptian position on his recent visit to Moscow.[38]

Images of Arab aggression and the "Soviet-Arab war machine" dominated Hadassah literature.

In the aftermath of the War of Independence in 1948, the United Nations established the United Nations Relief and Works Agency (UNRWA) to address the needs of Palestinian refugees and to resettle them in makeshift refugee camps built of mud huts. By the early 1950s, the issue of Palestinian refugees no longer received political attention, as the Arab host countries took responsibility, albeit often haphazardly, for the refugee.[39] UNRWA continued to maintain a presence in the camps.[40] After the 1967 War, a new wave of Palestinians moved into refugee camps. In addition, as Israel moved into the territories of the West Bank and Gaza, it also took control of 590,000 Palestinians in the West Bank and 380,000 in the Gaza strip.[41]

Hadassah leadership stressed that Arab refugees belonged in Arab countries. Dr. Miriam Freund, chair of the Zionist Affairs Committee, stated in a letter that was distributed in a Zionist Affairs kit:[42] "We deplore the reckless and irresponsible policies seeking to mobilize Arab refugees for a war against Israel, and for activities menacing the security of Israel's people. Accordingly this convention calls upon UNRWA to withhold rations from members of the army of the Palestinian Liberation Organization who are being trained for aggression against the people of a member state of the United Nations."[43]

Dr. Freund called upon Hadassah members to study the position of AIPAC on the Arab refugee issue. A Zionist Affairs Kit circulated to Hadassah chapters in November 1964 included a supplement on Arab propaganda influenced by AIPAC's description of "the Arab propaganda line." The supplement, Dr. Freund argued, "will help you to answer the assertions of Arab propagandists and of spokesmen who support the Arab line. It explains the methods used, the claims made, and supplies the facts."[44] The Zionist Affairs Committee chair designed the supplement as an item that specific members could order to inform themselves about the "Arab propaganda." [45]

To resist the negative press, Hadassah members could answer any attack with information provided in the supplement. In addition to reading the supplements for personal use, Hadassah members were asked to distribute these materials to libraries and to the community at large.[46] Among the many roles Hadassah members played, the role of spokespeople and defenders for Israel against criticism grew in importance, because of the increase in world criticism of Israel's positions. In order to provide a unified defense of Israel against what was perceived as a barrage of criticism, Hadassah members and its leadership developed a strict binary understanding of the Arab-Israeli conflict that painted good versus evil with no room for shades of gray. As the conflict continued to deepen over the next few decades, American

Jews in general, including Hadassah, found it problematic both to support Israel's existence and criticize certain aspects of its policy.

A letter from the chair of the Zionist Affairs Committee to the Hadassah members clarified the organization's position on the Arab refugee status. Counter to Arab assertions that the 1948 War dislocated one million Arab refugees, Hadassah argued that those numbers were greatly exaggerated and not based on any scientific assessment of the situation. In addition, Arab nations who invaded Israel in 1948, Hadassah explained, shared responsibility for any uprooting that did occur as a result of the war. Over 200,000 refugees had been successfully absorbed into the local communities of Syria and Lebanon, and Israel had absorbed another 140,000 Arabs into the state. It was also argued that many of the Palestinians had only briefly resided in Israel and therefore had no claim to Israeli land.[47]

Hadassah discourse grew more critical about the issue of refugees during the 1960s. By the post-1967 period, with a new world emphasis on the refugee problem, Hadassah publications, resolutions, kits, and seminars all focused on debunking "Arab propaganda" on the issue of refugees. One article in the *Philadelphia Chapter Hadassah News Bulletin* warned about the dangers King Hussein of Jordan posed to the Jewish people and to peace in general in the Middle East. The article called Hussein an anti-Semite who spewed hate messages toward Jews, and it noted that he refused to meet with Israel and demanded that the West Bank be returned to Jordan. Hussein "constantly refers to the cruel fate of the Arab refugees that has now grown in number by 200,000 as a result of Israel 'aggression.'" The article then goes on to quote Dr. Walter Pinner, who argued that the UN figures on refugees were greatly exaggerated. "It is the greatest misrepresentation ever perpetuated under the banner of the United Nations." In fact, Pinner contended that there existed more Jewish refugees from Arab countries in Israel than the whole total of Arab refugees in Arab countries.[48] "Every one of us," the article concluded, "must be well informed to answer accusations about the refugees."[49]

In the aftermath of the War for Independence, varying stories about the plight of Arab refugees surfaced. On January 23, 1967, Benjamin S. Rosenthal, a house representative from New York, brought to the floor of Congress Hadassah's message. He presented a five-point plan developed by the Park Hills Chapter of Hadassah in Queens, New York. Based on Hadassah resolutions and literature, the plan expressed Hadassah's position on Arab-Israel relations and the role of the United States in the Middle East. The plan called for the United States to maintain a balance of power in the region, urged the United States government to be more involved with a peace process, and supported aid to Arab counties for social and economic rather than military purposes. With regard to the issue of Arab refugees, the plan read to Congress by Representative Rosenthal stated:

> We reaffirm the conviction that the only logical solution to the Arab refugee problem is their resettlement in Arab lands. We submit that the United States should censure continuing efforts by Arab leaders to mobilize into an army to wage war against Israel. It is intolerable that UNRWA funds, contributed to refugee relief and rehabilitation, should be diverted to subsidize the Palestinian Liberation Army, which is organized for the destruction of Israel.[50]

The issue of Arab refugees had existed before 1967, and it was first raised in the aftermath of the War for Independence. After the Six-Day War, however, the dimensions of the problem expanded. *Hadassah Magazine* reported: "June, 1967 did not solve the Arab refugee problem but it did expose it. It is not a sociological problem nor economic — it is a political one. They are jobless and hungry, backward and uneducated. This has not been caused by us but is due to the fact that both East and West have not brought to bear the pressure."[51] The implication here was that the Arab refugee should not be Israel's problem but rather the world's issue.

Hadassah, along with most Jewish organizations, hotly contested the protests of Arab refugees and cast Arab nations as a negative force aligned with communists in a battle for democracy. Yet they also continued to stress the importance of keeping their services available to Arabs in both the West Bank and Israel proper. Holding true to their ideology of cultural pluralism and acceptance, Hadassah leaders and members attempted to reconcile a seemingly contradictory perspective on Arabs. On the one hand, articles, resolutions, and Hadassah literature painted Arabs as manipulative, misleading, violent, and aligned with

Communists. On the other hand, Hadassah maintained a policy of inclusion when it came to the Hadassah Medical Center in Jerusalem and various other Hadassah improvement projects. Events like the Six-Day War and its aftermath only complicated this tenuous approach.

A POST-1967 WORLD

Perceptions of Israel changed among the world community after 1967, as the view of Israel as an underdog was replaced by view of Israel as the aggressor. In the post-1967 period, Hadassah increasingly found itself defending Israeli policy and the very right for Israel to exist.[52] As discussed earlier in this book, Hadassah's approach toward civil rights issues and McCarthyism within the United States reflected this ideology of cultural pluralism. During the 1960s, Hadassah continued to extend medical care to Arabs within Israel and after the Six-Day War from the West Bank. In addition, Hadassah spearheaded other programs designed to bring Jews and Arabs together both in Israel and the United States. For example, in Neurim, Israel, Hadassah's Rural Vocational Center under the Youth Aliyah program and the Vocational Education Program, Hadassah offered courses to Arab youth as well as Jewish youth. Jewish students participated in a field trip to the nearby town of Acre where they met Arabs living in a "mixed city" where Arabs and Jews lived "side by side." This field trip exposed students to an urban Arab population and provided an avenue for cultural exchange.[53] Hadassah literature also expounded on the economic, social, and political benefits Arab citizens received in Israel. These included universal access to medical care, education, and education and freedom of religion.[54]

Inscribed at Hadassah's original Straus House in Jerusalem was the statement, "Service Without Distinction of Race or Creed."[55] Firsthand accounts of Arabs receiving service in Hadassah Medical Center portrayed the universal assistance the hospital provided to its Arab patients. One Hadassah article, entitled "Little Nasser at the Medical Center," reported the tale of a baby Arab boy accompanied by his mother who received life saving surgery. The report featured a picture of the happy mother and son.[56]

As relations between Arab nations, terrorist organizations, and the new population of the West Bank worsened, however, efforts to present Arabs in a positive light became more difficult. Rather than deny service to Arabs at the Hadassah Medical Center, Hadassah continued to serve the Arab and Palestinian population. In doing so, they proudly declared to the world and to themselves that Hadassah and Israel were a positive force in Arab lives. After the unification of Jerusalem, Hadassah Medical center admitted eighty to one hundred Arab patients a day — which amounted to 8 to 10 percent of their outpatients and 6 percent of their inpatients. In addition, Hadassah lowered its charges for many Arabs who could not afford the regular fees and turned no one away. Hadassah publications stressed the importance of this open-door policy and celebrated the positive function Hadassah played in the lives of residents of the West Bank.[57] A number of feature stories in the *Hadassah Magazine* and *Hadassah Newsletter* focused on personal stories of Arab patients of Hadassah.[58]

In her column "Diary of an Israeli Housewife" in October 1967, Molly Bar-David provided an account of a trip to the Gaza strip refugee camp. Responding to the concerns of an Arab doctor acquaintance who feared for his family in Gaza, Bar-David explained that she went to Gaza to show the doctor that in Israel, "the Arabs are as free as the Jews."[59] She told her readers that Gaza had been "wrenched" from Israel nineteen years previously and that now the Israeli flag was flying over it. The image of Arab "children dirty in rags" and men "loafing about in the shade, or piddling away on the relief jobs created by our government" reminded Bar -David of the Palestine she had known in 1937. The article then detailed the excellent provisions provided to the Arabs by UNWRA. More than anything, Bar-David warned that Arabs had been fed "hatred towards the Jews" through Egyptian and Nazi propaganda. Israel, Bar-David explained, supported Arab refugees, even though the Arabs hate Jews.[60]

Changing attitudes toward Israel on the part of the world at large, coupled with a reexamination of the relationship between the Diaspora and Israel during the 1960s, forced Hadassah to contend with new questions about the role of Zionism in the American Jewish community. In response to comments by Israeli Prime Minister Ben

Gurion, indicating that the Zionist movement no longer held great importance because of the establishment and success of the State of Israel, Rose Halprin, former national president of Hadassah, stated at the 1960 Hadassah national convention:

> He compares the movement to the "scaffolding of a building" and suggests that now that the building is complete, the scaffolding must come down. He is in error in the analogy he draws. The Zionist movement was never the "scaffolding." Rather, it was the integral part of the building itself. We helped lay the foundation stone. We are a retaining wall. A builder who breaks such a wall does so at peril to the safety of the building itself. And, so we answer "No" to Mr. Ben Gurion not because we have vested interests, but because we — as he — are custodians of Jewish history and responsible for Jewish survival.[61]

Halprin further explained that the Zionist movement served to bind American Jews to their culture and to secure both the prosperity of the State of Israel and the survival of the Jewish people.[62] In the 1960s, Hadassah sought to ensure the relevance of Zionist activity to American Jews. A relationship with Israel and Zionism would act as a bridge between American Jews and Israel — as well as a bridge to thousands of years of history and culture.[63]

At the same conference, Hadassah adopted a resolution affirming its commitment to perpetuating a strong Zionist movement. The resolution outlined the responsibilities of Zionists in the United States. Among them were: to improve the relationship between Jews within and without Israel, to educate Jewish youth in Israel and the Diaspora about their Jewish heritage, and to teach Hebrew to and to inform the American people about issues concerning Israel. [64]

In addition, Hadassah aggressively defended the importance of Zionism against criticism both from within the Jewish community and from anti-Zionist Jewish groups like the American Council for Judaism. There was criticism from the Arab world, and a growing public discourse in the United States identified Israel as an aggressive imperial presence in the Middle East.

Widespread anxiety over the level of preparedness of Jewish youth and college students to defend Israel and the ideology of Zionism against criticism prompted Hadassah to engage in various education campaigns. Hadassah distributed kits to Jewish high school and college age students. The kits addressed issues concerning Arabs in Israel and Arab refugees, the American Council for Judaism, and Israel and the international scene.[65] The Denver Chapter of Hadassah held a one-day seminar for high school seniors who, although apparently scholastically prepared to face the outside world, were "not sufficiently prepared and knowledgeable enough to explain Judaism, Israel and the position of the American Jews to their inquiring non-Jewish friends."[66]

UNITED NATIONS

Although Hadassah challenged the status of Arabs as refugees and critiqued UN involvement in this issue, the organization supported many UN programs. Hadassah had aligned itself with the United Nations in the 1950s, and they continued to affiliate throughout the 1960s. Hadassah leaders viewed the United Nations as an objective organization that served global interest and promoted world peace. The United Nations had played a central role in the establishment of the State of Israel, and throughout the 1950s and increasingly in the 1960s, Hadassah members looked toward the United Nations as a stabilizing force in a volatile Cold War world. Hadassah served as an NGO affiliated with the Public Information Department of the United Nations, and it both educated and lobbied its members and political officials about the importance of supporting the United Nations. Hadassah chapters promoted UNICEF programs by selling UN greeting cards, and they supplied information pamphlets about the history of the United Nations to social studies high school classes. In addition, courses were designed to educate Hadassah members about the importance of the United Nations.[67]

At the 1960 Hadassah annual convention in New York, Hadassah passed a resolution stating the organization's support for the United Nations as an "instrument set up to guard against the calamity of war and to establish the rule of law and peace among nations." It also defined the United Nations as an organization working "toward the obliteration of disease, illiteracy and poverty." The resolution urged the U.S. government to "exert leadership in the United Nations, by encouraging maximum use of the vast machinery of the United Nations."[68] Hadassah passed similar resolutions in annual conferences throughout the early 1960s.

In an effort to better inform members, American Affairs kits included coverage of UN issues and updates. Hadassah appointed a UN liaison, Mrs. Arthur Ellis, and an alternate, to attend briefings held by the U.S. mission to the United Nations. Ellis also provided information on current UN issues and programs to the organization.[69]

Hadassah championed the UN adoption in 1966 of the International Convention on the Elimination of all Forms of Racial Discrimination. In an American Affairs kit distributed in January of 1966, the matter was explained: "after condemning racial segregation, apartheid and all who espouse them,"[70] the United Nations established a committee that would "have authority to hear complaints from one nation about racial discrimination of another and a complicated system permits the committee to appoint a group to look into the complaint, hear testimony from all parties, and make suggestions for amelioration of outstanding problems."[71] Later that year, another kit explained that the term *racism* also "was broad enough" to include anti-Semitism.[72]

Hadassah further articulated its approval of UN programs by resolutions passed in 1966 and 1967 urging the United States to "take prompt action to ratify" several conventions already passed by the United Nations, including the Convention on Genocide, the Abolition of Enforced Labor, the Abolition of Slavery, the Political Rights of Women, and the Convention on the Elimination of all Forms of Racial Discrimination. Hadassah couched its support for these "human rights" conventions by invoking the Jewish tradition of social justice. "We hold these conventions to be vital factors in furthering American and Jewish ideals of universal freedom and the development of a social order based on reason, justice and equality."[73]

Prior to 1967, Hadassah rhetoric wholeheartedly accepted that the United Nations served as an international group to deter war and implement peaceful resolutions to international conflict. After 1967, however, Hadassah shifted its thinking about the United Nations as an arm for peacekeeping and focused primarily on the United Nations' commitment to social welfare and human rights. In a 1966 resolution, Hadassah argued that because it was underfunded and disorganized, the United Nations failed "to bring peace" to the world but instead "effected an absence of war." By 1967 and the outbreak of the war in the Middle East, Hadassah viewed the actions of the United Nations as weak and ineffectual. "The peace keeping machinery of the United Nations Expeditionary force, set up after the 1956 Sinai campaign, seemed unable to function as an active force for peace, since when Egypt requested the UNEF be withdrawn, the Secretary-General felt himself committed to accede to the request of the sovereign power — Egypt — on whose land the UNEF had been placed."[74] Hadassah leaders also believed that the politics of block voting within the United Nations and the "power-play" of various member nations had the potential to favor Arab nations over Israel.[75] Hadassah continued to support the United Nations as a place to resolve foreign policy issues, but it dampened its enthusiasm for the objectivity and efficiency of the United Nations as a force for peace.

SOVIET JEWRY

Another area in which Hadassah engaged in foreign policy during the 1960s was that of concern for Soviet Jewry. The president of Hadassah, Mrs. Kramarsky, at the 1964 annual convention in Los Angeles, spoke of the importance of Jews in general and Hadassah members in particular to the fight for freedom for Soviet Jewry. She warned that anti-Semitism remained a powerful force in the world. Jews in Russia, for example, were "denied the natural and inalienable right of all people to practice their religion and to teach it to their children."[76] Mrs. Kramarsky went on to detail the ways in which Hadassah and other Jewish organizations had mobilized for this effort. The "world must know beyond any doubt that 'we are our brother's keepers.'"[77] Kramarsky delineated a platform of action in alliance with other Jewish organizations with the purpose of awakening the American government to the severity of the situation and convincing them to act on behalf of Jews by influencing the USSR to eliminate its anti-Semitic policies.[78] Mrs. Max Schenk of New York, the chairperson of the conference, warned of the "spiritual genocide" and "cultural obliteration" that threatened "all Jews falling under the yoke of Communism."[89]

Hadassah worked to assist Jews living under Soviet oppression. In a resolution about Soviet anti-Semitism passed at the Los Angeles National Convention in 1964, Hadassah voiced its concern for the Jews of the USSR. Hadassah, "vigorously protests the calculated assaults against the cultural and spiritual life of the Jews within the Soviet Union. Our aim is to mobilize American public opinion into a moral force and to arouse our government to exert its influence to the end that this unconscionable wrong will be righted. We urge also that the Soviet government permit Jewish Families to reunite with their families abroad."[80] The resolution went on to express Hadassah's support for the resolution condemning Soviet anti-Semitism introduced into Congress by Senator Abraham Ribicoff from Connecticut.[81]

The protection of Soviet Jewry from its perceived near extinction served as another cause that made Hadassah women feel themselves to be important and essential members of the Jewish community. As so much of the membership materials, it expressed Hadassah's underlying goal of self-empowerment: "Hadassah makes you important." In August 1965, on behalf of Hadassah, the organization sent a letter to Mme. M. D. Ovsyannikova, the editor in chief of *Sovietskaya Zmenshchina* (*The Soviet Woman*). The letter pleaded with Soviet women "as women to women" to allow Jewish children to receive a Jewish education and learn about their heritage and culture.[82] Hadassah further made its case in a resolution adopted at the national convention in August 1966 in Boston:

> On behalf of its 300,000 members Hadassah calls on the Government of The United States to exert maximum influence within the United Nations and through diplomatic channels to convince the Soviet government that discriminatory policies against Jewish Nationals constituted a violation of elementary human rights, which are a common concern of free men and nations.[83]

In other parts of the world, Hadassah hoped to provide guidance to developing countries. While some parts of the African community viewed Israel as an imperialist foreign presence, during the 1960s, Hadassah expanded its medical programs to include humanitarian programs to aid African counties in improving their medical facilities and programs. In Liberia, for example, Hadassah aided in the establishment of an ophthalmology center by sending doctors and staff to oversee the creation of the unit. In addition, nurses and doctors visited and trained at Hadassah medical facilities in Israel. Hadassah also offered free\medical schooling to Ethiopian students. In addition, Hadassah offered free services to certain emergency cases in Ethiopia.[84]

Hadassah continued to articulate the importance of Hadassah members as the protectors of Jews and Jewish culture in the 1960s. While American Affairs emphasized the work to be accomplished within the United States and on the domestic front, Hadassah's very existence rested on calling Jewish women to action that was political, cultural, and philanthropic, based on the notion that as women, they were uniquely situated to protect and nurture Jews everywhere. In addition, instead of stressing traditional forms of women's roles within Judaism that may have stressed synagogue attendance and child rearing, Hadassah formulated a new identity for Jewish women that made Jewish women's action imperative to the survival of the Jewish people.

ENDNOTES

Introduction

1. Judith Butler, *Gender Trouble* (New York: Routledge, 1999).

2. Mary McCune, The Whole Wide World, Without Limits: International Relief, Gender Politics, and American Jewish Women, 1893–1930. (Detroit: Wayne State University Press, 2005), 23.

3. Mary McCune, The Whole, 26.

4. Mary McCune, The Whole, 24.

5. Mira Katzburg-Yungman, "Women and Zionist Activity in Erez Israel: The Case of Hadassah, 1913–1958 in Shulamit Reinharz and Mark A. Raider, eds., *American Jewish Women and The Zionist Enterprise* (Waltham: Brandeis University Press, 2005),165.

6. For more on this see: Nancy Hewitt, ed. *No Permanent Waves: Recasting Histories of U.S Feminism* (New Brunswick: Rutgers University Press, 2010) and Kathleen Laughlin and Jacqueline Castledine, eds. *Breaking the Wave: Women, Their Organizations, and Feminism, 1945–1985* (New York: Routledge, 2011).

7. Mira Katzburg-Yungman, "Women," 164.

8. Yaffa Schlesinger, "Hadassah, the National Women's Zionist Organization of America," *Contemporary Jewry* 15, 121–139; Naomi Lichtenberg, "Hadassah's Founders and Palestine, 1912–1925: A Quest for Meaning and the Creation of Women's Zionism" (PhD dissertation, Indiana, 1995); Marvin Levin, *It Takes a Dream: The Story of Hadassah* (New York: Gefen Publishing, 1997); Sandra Berliant Kadosh, "Ideology vs. Reality: Youth Aliyah and the Rescue of Jewish Children During the Holocaust, 1933–1945" (PhD dissertation, Columbia University, 1995).

9. Deborah Dash Moore, *To the Golden Cities: Pursuing the American Dream in Miami and Los Angeles* (New York: Free Press, 1994), 17.

10. Mary McCune, "Social Workers in the *Muskeljudentum*: 'Hadassah Ladies,' 'Manly Men' and the Significance of Gender in the American Zionist Movement 1912–1928," *American Jewish History* 86, no. 2 (June 1998): 135–165.

11. June Sochen, "Both the Dove and the Serpent: Hadassah's Work in 1920s," *Judaism* 52, no. 1/2 (Winter 2003): 71–83; Lichtenberg, "Hadassah's Founders and Palestine."

12. Schlesinger, "Hadassah, The National Women's Zionist."

13. Donald Miller, "A History of Hadassah 1912–1935" (PhD dissertation, New York

University, 1968). Balia Round Shargel, "American Jewish Women in Palestine: Bessie Gotsfeld, Henrietta Szold, and the Zionist Enterprise," *American Jewish History* 90 (June 2002): 141–161. Sandra Berliant Kadosh, "Ideology vs. Reality: Youth Aliyah and the Rescue of Jewish Children During the Holocaust, 1933–1945" (PhD dissertation, Columbia University, 1995). Balia Round Shargel, *Lost Love: the Untold Story of Henrietta Szold Unpublished Diaries and Letters* (Philadelphia: Jewish Publication Society, 1997). Irving Fineman, *Woman of Valor: the Life of Henrietta Szold* (New York: Simon Schuster, 1961).

14. Roberta Hanfling Schwartz, "Henrietta Szold Meets Glukel of Hamelm," *Judaism* 51, no. 2 (Spring 2002): 201–213.

15. Michael Brown, "Henrietta Szold's Progressive American Vision of the Yishuv," in Allon Gal, ed., *Envisioning Israel* (Jerusalem: Magnes Press, 1996).

16. Irving Fineman, *Woman of Valor: the Life of Henrietta Szold* (New York: Simon Schuster, 1961), 342.

17. Shulamit Magnus, "'Out of the Ghetto': Integrating the Study of Jewish Women into the Study of Jews," *Judaism* 39, no. 1 (1990): 28–36; Susannah Heschel, "Women's Studies," *Modern Judaism* 10 (1990): 243–258. For a more recent analysis, see Robin Judd, "Religion, Agency and Power in Jewish Gender Studies," *Journal of Women's History* 15 (Spring 2003): 227.

18. I first identified this strain of Americanism and civic activism in Hadassah rhetoric in my 2005 dissertation, "Not Just Ladies That Lunch: Hadassah and the Formation of a Jewish Women's Consciousness in Post–World War II America" (PhD dissertation, University of Southern California, 2005), and in two subsequent articles, Shirli Brautbar, "Fashioning Gender and Jewishness: Hadassah, Fashion Shows, and Beauty Culture in the Post World War II Era," *Dress*, V. 33, 2006 and Shirli Brautbar, "Hadassah's Ideological Rhetoric In the Post World War II Era," *National Social Science Journal*, V. 32 No. 1, 2009. Graduate student Rebecca Boim Wolf later addressed some of themes in an essay, "It's Good Americanism: Selling Hadassah in the Postwar Era" in Hasia Diner, Shira Kohn, and Rachel Kranson, eds. *Jewish Feminine Mystique?: Jewish Women in Postwar America* (New Brunswick: Rutgers University Press: Oct. 2010).

19. Elaine Tyler May, *Homeward Bound: American Families in the Cold War Era* (New York: Basic Books, 1988).

20. Leila Rupp and Verta Taylor, *Survival in the Doldrums: The American Women's Rights Movement, 1945 to the 1960s* (New York: Oxford University Press, 1987), 6.

21. Rupp and Taylor, *Survival in the Doldrums*, 7, 8.

22. Susan Levine, *Degrees of Equality* (Philadelphia: Temple University Press, 1995), 67.

23. Levine, *Degrees*, 67.

24. Levine, *Degrees*, 77.

25. Levine, *Degrees*.

26. Lois Banner, *American Beauty* (New York: Knopf, 1983).

27. Joanne Meyerowitz, "Beyond the Feminine Mystique: A Reassessment of Post-War Mass Culture, 1946–1958" in Meyerowitz, ed., *Not June Cleaver; Women and Gender in Post-War America* (Philadelphia, Temple University Press, 1994).

28.   Elaine Tyler May, *Homeward Bound: American Families on the Cold War* (New York: Basic Books, 1988); Meyerowitz, *June Cleaver*; Nancy Walker, "Humor and Gender Roles: The 'Funny' Feminism of the Post–World War II Suburbs," *American Quarterly* 37 (1985): 99–113; Wini Breines, *Young White and Miserable: Growing Up Female in the Fifties* (Chicago: University Chicago Press, 2001); Jessamyn Nuehaus, "The Way to a Man's Heart: Gender Roles, Domestic Ideology, and Cookbooks in the 1950s," *Journal of Social History* (Spring 19): 529–555; Susan Douglas, *Where the Girls Are: Growing Up Female with the Mass Media* (New York: Times Books, 1994); Elizabeth Kennedy and Madeline Davis, *Boots of Leather, Slippers of Gold: A History of a Lesbian Community* (New York: Routledge, 1993); Lynn Spiegel, *Welcome to the Dream House: Popular Media and Postwar Suburbs* (Durham, NC: Duke University Press, 2001).

29.   Anne Frior Scott, *Natural Allies: Women's Associations in American History* (Chicago: University of Illinois, 1991), 2. For more on women's organizations, see also Ruth Bordin, *Women and Temperance: The Quest for Power and Liberty* (New Brunswick, NJ: Rutgers University Press, 1990); Kenneth D. Rose, *American Women and the Repeal of Prohibition* (New York: New York University Press, 1996); Caryn Neumann, "The End of Gender Solidarity: The History of the Women's Organization for National Prohibition Reform in the United States, 1929–1933," *Journal of Women's History* 19, no. 2 (summer 1997): 31–51.

30.   Joyce Antler, "Between Culture and Politics: The Emma Lazarus Federation of Jewish Women's Clubs and the Promulgation of Women's History, 1944–1989," in Vicki Ruiz and Ellen Carol Dubois, eds., *Unequal Sisters,* 3rd edition (New York: Routledge, 2000).

31.   Faith Rogow, *Gone to Another Meeting: The National Council of Jewish Women* (Birmingham: University of Alabama Press, 1993); Deborah Dash Moore, *B'nai B'rith and the Challenge of Ethnic Leadership* (Albany: State University of New York, 1981), 195.

32.   Rogow, *Gone.* Also on NCJW, see Seth Korelitz, "A Magnificent Piece of Work": The Americanization Work of the National Council of Jewish Women," *American Jewish History* 83 (1995): 177–203.

33.   Jacob Marcus, *The American Jewish Woman, 1654–1980* (New York: Ktav, 1981), 143.

34.   Hasia Diner and Beryl Lieff Benderly, *Her Works Praise Her: A History of Jewish Women in America from Colonial Times to the Present* (New York: Basic Books, 2002); Charlotte Baum, Paula Hyman, and Sonya Michael, *The Jewish Woman in America* (New York: New American Library, 1975); Sochen, *Consecrate Every Day.* For an oral history approach, see Joyce Antler, *The Journey Home: Jewish Women and the American Century* (New York: The Free Press, 1997); Hyman and Moore, *Jewish Women in America*; Marcus, *Jewish American Woman.*

35.   Arthur A. Goren, *The Politics and Public Culture of American Jews* (Indiana University Press, 1999), 192.

36.   Naomi Cohen, "Zionism as Liberalism," in Gal, *Envisioning Israel,* 320.

37.   Cohen, "Zionism as Liberalism," 321.

38.   Jerold Auerbach, *Are We One?: Jewish Identity in the United States and Israel* (New Brunswick: Rutgers University Press, 2001), 65; Marcus, *American Jewish Woman,* 92.

39.   As quoted in "History of the Boston Hadassah Chapter," 1, call no. 5, box 6, "Jubilee 25th" folder, HA.

40. "History of the Boston Hadassah Chapter," 2; "The Chicago Chapter Silver Jubilee," 6; Goldreich, *The Hadassah Idea*, 13.

41. "Hadassah Manual 1957–1958," 5, 12, HA.

42. "Hadassah Manual 1957–1958," 6.

43. Charles Hoffman, *The Smoke Screen* (Savage: Eshel Books, 1989), 93.

Chapter I

1. "A New Judea is Born: Jews are Jubilant – Arabs Threaten Peace Haganah Called Into Action," *The Senior* January 1948, 1, located in call no.17, Hadassah Archives (HA), Center for Jewish History, New York.

2. The term *Palestine* connotes the prestate period and was the wording used by members of Hadassah. Later after statehood, the term *Israel* is used.

3. Jerold Auerbach, *Are We One?: Jewish Identity in the United States and Israel* (New Brunswick, Rutgers University Press, 2001), 52. On liberalism, also see Arthur Goren, *The Politics and Public Culture of American Jews* (Bloomington: Indiana University Press, 1999).

4. Auerbach, 82.

5. Michael Brown, *The Israeli American Connection: Its Roots in the Yishuv 1914-1945* (Detroit: Wayne State University Press, 1996); Naomi Lichtenberg, "Hadassah's Founders and Palestine, 1912–1925: A Quest for Meaning and the Creation of Women's Zionism" (PhD dissertation, Indiana University, 1995).

6. Mary McCune, "Social Workers in the *Muskeljudentum*: 'Hadassah Ladies,' 'Manly Men' and the Significance of Gender in the American Zionist movement 1912–1928," *American Jewish History* 86, no. 2 (June 1998):

7. See also Mary McCune, *The Whole Wide World, Without Limits International Relief, Gender Politics, and American Jewish Women, 1893-1930* (Wayne State University Press, 2005).

8. McCune, "Social Workers," 138.

9. In addition, the focus of this book will be on the activities and cultural images and perceptions of the American population. While Hadassah had great political and philanthropic impact in Palestine, several historians have already provided great insight to that.

10. Paula Hyman, *Gender and Assimilation in Modern Jewish History: The Roles and Representations of Women* (University of Washington Press, 1995), 26.

11. Herbert Biskla Morris, "A History of the Jewish Centers Association of Los Angeles with Special Reference to Jewish Identity" (master's thesis, University Southern California, 1972); Eveyln Bodek, "Making Do: Jewish Women and Philanthropy," in *Jewish Life in Philadelphia* (ISHI Publications, 1983); Anne Baude, "Jewish Women in the Twentieth Century Building a Life in America," in Rosemary Reuther and Rosemary Skinner Keller, eds., *Women and Religion in America*, vol. 3 (Harper and Row, 1986); Faith Rogow, *Gone to Another Meeting* (University of Alabama Press, 1993); June Sochen, *Consecrate Every Day: The Public Lives of Everyday Women* (State University of New York Press, 1981).

11. Henrietta Szold letter to Elvira Solis, January 18, 1918, in Marlin Lowenthal, *Henrietta Szold Life and Letters* (New York: Viking Press, 1942), 102.

12. Aaron Berman, *Nazism, the Jews and American Zionism 1933–1945* (Wayne State University Press, 1990), 35.

13. Berman, *Nazism*, 11.

14. Berman, *Nazism*, 12.

15. Berman, *Nazism*, 120; Penkower, *The Holocaust and Israel Reborn* (University of Illinois Press, 1994), 12.

16. Melvin Urofsky, *American Zionism from Herzl to the Holocaust* (Lincoln, University of Nebraska Press, 1995), 21.

17. Berman, *Nazism*; Penkower, *The Holocaust*, 12

18. Berman, *Nazism*, 34.

19. Sandra Berliant Kadosh, "Ideology vs. Reality: Youth Aliyah and the Rescue of Jewish Children During the Holocaust, 1933–1945" (PhD dissertation, Columbia University, 1995), 5.

20. "Why I Belong to Hadassah," brochure, 1, in call no. 17, box 8, "1940s" folder, HA.

21. "Why I Belong to Hadassah," 2.

23. "Jewish State Is Born," *Hadassah Headlines*, December 1947, 1.

24. Moshe Shertok, "Statehood Needed for Further Growth," *Hadassah Newsletter*, December 1947, 8.

25. Jean Jacobson, Oral History, published in *A Tapestry of Hadassah Memories*, Miriam Freund Rosenthal, ed. (The Town House Press, 1994), 116.

26. "5000 at Hadassah Convention Pledge Support for Jewish State" *Hadassah Newsletter*, December 1947, 1.

27. "5000 at Hadassah Convention," 1.

28. "Mobilize For the Jewish State through Hadassah" *Hadassah Headlines*, February 1948, 6.

29. "5000 at Hadassah Convention," 1.

30. Shertok, "Statehood Needed for Future Growth," 8.

31. "Political Kits Merit Widest Circulation: Public Relations Drive Must Be Intensified," *Hadassah Headlines*, August 1948, 6.

32. "Political Line Must also Talk Emergency," *Hadassah Headlines*, February 1948, 8.

33. Jean Jacobson, Oral History, 116.

34. Jean Jacobson, Oral History, 117.

35. "Political Line Must also Talk Emergency," *Hadassah Headlines*, February 1948, 8.

36. "Political Kits Merit Widest Circulation: Public Relations Drive Must Be Intensified," *Hadassah Headlines*, August 1948, 6.

37. Hadassah, "Hadassah to 'Hold Largest Convention in its History," press release, 14 October 1948, in call no. 3, box 14, folder 3, HA.

28. Lichtenberg, "Hadassah's Founders."

39. Hadassah members used their husband's names at this point in Hadassah history. That

started to change in the 1960s, when Hadassah members started to use their own first names.

40. "Hadassah Rallies for Security," *Hadassah Newsletter*, Jan 1948, 1; "National Board Mobilizes for Medical Defense," *Hadassah Newsletter*, January 1948, 1.

41. "Hadassah to 'Hold Largest Convention,'" press release.

42. "Hadassah to 'Hold Largest Convention,'" press release.

43. "Resolutions Adopted by the Thirty-fourth Annual Convention of Hadassah, the Women's Zionist Organization of America," 5–9 November 1948, 1, in call no. 3, box no. 14, folder no. 4, HA.

44. "Resolutions Adopted," 3.

45. "Resolutions Adopted," 19.

46. "Resolutions Adopted," 19.

47. See Lichtenberg, "Hadassah's Founders," for a full treatment of this issue.

48. Henrietta Szold, letter to Bertha Landsman, 28 August 1923, in Associate Correspondence Series, HA, as quoted in Lichtenberg, "Hadassah's Founders," 69.

49. "The Jewish State and Hadassah," *Hadassah Newsletter*, January 1948, 2.

50. "The Jewish State and Hadassah, 2.

51. Goren, *The Politics*, 172.

52. Goren, *The Politics*, 182.

53. "1949 Resolutions adopted,"5, in call no. 3, box 15, folder 5, HA.

54. Goren, *The Politics*, 178

55. Brown, *The Israeli American*, 134–135.

56. Brown, *The Israeli American*, 139.

57. Lichtenberg, "Hadassah's Founders," 41, 42.

58. Lichtenberg, "Hadassah's Founders," 76.

59. Lichtenberg, "Hadassah's Founders," 47.

60. Henrietta Szold, letter to Mrs. Rebekah Schweitzer, April 14, 1921, in Associate Correspondence Series, HA, as quoted in Lichtenberg, "Hadassah's Founders," 47.

61. "UN Votes Jewish State," 1.

62. Found both in *Hadassah Headlines* March 1948, 5, and *Hadassah Newsletter* March 1948, 1.

63. Found both in *Hadassah Headlines* March 1948, 5, and *Hadassah Newsletter* March 1948, 1.

64. Found both in *Hadassah Headlines* March 1948, 5, and *Hadassah Newsletter* March 1948, 1.

65. *Hadassah Newsletter*, April 1948, 2.

66. *Hadassah Newsletter*, April 1948, 2.

67. *Hadassah Newsletter*, April 1948, 2.

68. "Mobilize for the Jewish State through Hadassah," *Hadassah Headlines*, February 1948, 6.

69. "Mobilize for the Jewish State," 6.

70. "These Rosh Hashanah Cards Commemorate Jewish State," *Hadassah Headlines*, June 1949, 6.

71. A more extensive analysis of images of Israeli settlers will appear in chapter 2.

72. "Hadassah Serves Arab Children," *Hadassah Newsletter*, November 1949, 4.

73. "Fair Deal for Arabs in Israel's Program," *Hadassah Newsletter*, February 1950, 10.

74. Ian Ross MacFarlane, dispatch, 4 March 1947, in "Arabs treated at Hadassah HMO" folder, HA.

75. *Hadassah Mainline* 1, no. 1 (February 1949): n.p.

76. Esther Kesselman, Oral History, published in *A Tapestry of Hadassah Memories*, Miriam Freund Rosenthal, ed. (The Town House Press, 1994), 120.

77. "Diary of a Jerusalem Housewife," *Hadassah Newsletter*, September 1948, 5.

78. Esther Kesselman, Oral History, 120.

79. Benny Morris, *The Birth of the Palestinian Refugee Problem Revisited* (Cambridge University Press, 2003).

Chapter II

1. Gloria Goldreich Horowitz, *The Hadassah Idea: History and Development*, booklet (New York: Hadassah, 1968); "1968–1969 Annual Report," 19, in call no. 3, box 28, folder 2, Hadassah Archive (HA), Center for Jewish History, New York.

2. Hadassah, *Face toward the Future*, booklet (New York: Hadassah, October 1953), 14.

3. "Facts about Hadassah," 1966.

4. Hadassah, *Face toward the Future*, 18; "Facts about Hadassah," 1966.

5. Hadassah, *Face toward the Future*, 25.

6. Hadassah, *Face toward the Future*, 26.

7. "Hadassah 1968–1969 Annual Report," call no. 3, box 28, folder 2, HA.

8. "Facts about Hadassah," 1956, call no. 17, box 10, HA.

9. "Hadassah 1968–1969 Annual Report."

10. As quoted in Patterson, Clifford and Hagan, *American Foreign*, 289.

11. Jon Kimche, "Can Israel Help Defend the Middle East," *Hadassah Headlines*, February 1951, 5.

12. Kimche, "Can Israel," 5; "Sputnik and Other Russia Gains Place New Demand for Positive US Program in the Mid-East," *Hadassah Headlines*, November 1957, 2.

13. "Sputnik and Other," 2.

14. Howard M. Sachar, *The History of Israel from the Rise of Zionism to Our Time* (New York: Alfred Knopf, 1996), 474.

15. Sachar, *History of Israel*, 475.

16. Sachar, *History of Israel*, 474.

17. Avi Shalim, *The Iron Wall: Israel and the Arab World* (New York: W. W. Norton &

Company, 200), 162; Sachar, *The History*, 482.

18. Rose l. Halprin, "Suez Debate Is Test of Allied Unity," *Hadassah Newsletter*, October 1956, 1.

19. Halprin, "Suez Debate," 1.

20. *Hadassah Newsletter*, November 1956, n.p.

21. Joan Comay, "Eyewitness Report from Israel," *Hadassah Newsletter*, November 1956, 5.

22. Comay, "Eyewitness Report from Israel," 5.

23. Alfred Lilienthal, *The Zionist Connection* (NJ: North American, 1982), 537.

24. Patterson, Clifford and Hagan, *American Foreign*, 357.

25. Judith Epstein, interview by Miriam Freund, 3–4, in call no. 20, box 9, folder 5, HA.

26. Judith Epstein, interview by Miriam Freund, 3–4, in call no. 20, box 9, folder 5, HA.

27. Epstein interview.

28. Patterson, Clifford and Hagan, *American Foreign*, 332.

29. "Hadassah a Bulwark against Communism," *Hadassah Newsletter*, October 1955, 2.

30. "Hadassah a Bulwark against Communism," *Hadassah Newsletter*, October 1955, 2.

31. Faye Scenck, "Israel Is Not Alone," *Hadassah Newsletter,* November 1956, 9; Lilienthal, *Zionist Connection,* 535.

32. The same thing could be said for Jewish cultural issues. Many of the most prominent names in the Jewish community spoke at functions and published articles through Hadassah.

33. I first identified this strain of Americanism and civic activism in Hadassah rhetoric in my 2005 dissertation, "Not Just Ladies That Lunch: Hadassah and the Formation of a Jewish Women's Consciousness in Post–World War II America" (PhD dissertation, University of Southern California, 2005), and in two subsequent articles, Shirli Brautbar, "Fashioning Gender and Jewishness: Hadassah, Fashion Shows, and Beauty Culture in the Post World War II Era." *Dress,* v. 33, 2006 and Shirli Brautbar, "Hadassah's Ideological Rhetoric in the Post World War II Era," *National Social Science Journal,* v. 32 no. 1, 2009. Graduate student Rebecca Boim Wolf later addressed some of these themes in an essay, "It's Good Americanism: Selling Hadassah in the Postwar Era" in *Jewish Feminine Mystique?* eds. Hasia Diner, Shira Kohn, and Rachel Kranson: *Jewish Women in Postwar America* (New Brunswick: Rutgers University Press, October 2010).

34. "I Am a Neighbor of Yours: May I Come In," brochure, call no. 17, box no. 8, "1940s" folder, HA.

35. "Resolutions Adopted," 19; "Political Session, 34th Annual Hadassah Convention," press release, 7 November 1948, in call no. 3, box 14, folder 3, HA; "Excerpts From the Remarks of Mrs. David Greenberg at the Friday Evening Session of Hadassah," 5 November 1948, call no. 3, box 14, folder 6, HA.

36. I will explore issues of McCarthyism and the Cold War more fully in later chapters.

37. *Hadassah Newsletter,* September 1948, 9.

38. On dual allegiance, see Aurebach, *Are We One.*

39. "Our Six Paneled Exhibit Tells Hadassah Story: Can Be Used for Chapters and

Communities," *Hadassah Headlines*, November 1948, 1.

40. "Our Six Paneled Exhibit," 1.

41. *Shoreline Newsletter* 3, no. 4, December 1956, 3, in HA.

42. *Sarah Kuzzy Group Founding Newsletter*, 1953, in call no. 15, box 9, HA.

43. "Chapters Back AAUN Tour of Congressman Giving UN Data," *Hadassah Headlines*, April 1958, n.p.

44. "No 'Jim Crow' in Israel Arabs Enjoy Full Equality," *Hadassah Newsletter*, December 1950, 7.

45. "No 'Jim Crow'," 7.

46. "Bulletin," *Hadassah Shoreline* 1, no. 6, February 1955, 2.

47. "Homes for Arab Nomads," *Hadassah Newsletter*, June 1955, 15.

48. Mishna Cohen, "The Arab Minority in Israel," *Hadassah Newsletter*, July 1959, 5.

49. State of Israel, *The Arabs in Israel* (n.p.: Israel Government, 1955), 22.

50. "Oh You Know That," *Hadassah Shoreline* 3, no. 3, November 1956, 2.

51. "Oh You Know That," 2.

52. *Hadassah Shoreline* 3, no. 9, May 1957, n.p.

53. Frieda G. Shure, Oral History, 228.

54. Deborah Dash Moore, *To the Golden Cities: Pursuing the American Dream in Miami and Los Angeles* (Free Press, NY: 1994), 276.

55. Michael Berkowitz, *Zionist Culture and West European Jewry before the First World War* (Chapel Hill: The University of North Carolina Press, 1993).

56. Leon Uris, *Exodus* (Garden City, NY: Doubleday, 1958), 55.

Chapter III

1. "Hadassah 1968–1969 Annual Report," call no. 3, box 28, folder 2, Hadassah Archives at the American Jewish Historical Society housed at the Center for Jewish History, New York, NY (hereafter HA).

2. Whitfield, *Culture of Cold War* (Baltimore: Johns Hopkins University Press, 1996), 38.

3. Levine, *Degrees of Equality* (Philadelphia: Temple University Press, 1995).

4. Shirli Brautbar. "'Not Just Ladies That Lunch': Hadassah and the Formation of American Jewish Identity." PhD dissertation, University of Southern California, 2005.

5. "American Affairs Policy Adopted at Conference," *Hadassah Headlines*, January 1950, 7.

6. "US Must Destroy McCarthyism at Home and Work in Concert with Free Nations Abroad to Justify Position of Supremacy," press release, 18 September 1951, 1, in call no. 3, box 16, folder 5, HA.

7. "US Must Destroy McCarthyism," 1.

8. Howard Mumford Jones, "American Democratic Tradition," *Hadassah Newsletter*, November 1953, 4.

9. Howard Mumford Jones, "American Democratic Tradition," *Hadassah Newsletter*,

November 1953, 4.

10. "Minutes from Conference 1954," Call no. 3, box 18, folder 4, HA.

11. "Minutes from Conference 1954," Call no. 3, box 18, folder 4, HA.

12. Osmond K. Franekel, "The Anatomy of the Fifth Amendment," *Hadassah Newsletter*, January 1954, 2.

13. Patrick Murphy Malin, "Let's Look At the First Amendment," *Hadassah Newsletter*, January 1954, 1.

14. Jacob Javits, "A Congressman Looks at Congressional Investigation," *Hadassah Newsletter*, March 1954, 1.

15. Javits, "A Congressman Looks," 1.

16. "Hadassah a Bulwark," 2.

17. Shirli Brautbar. "'Not Just Ladies That Lunch': Hadassah and the Formation of American Jewish Identity." PhD dissertation, University of Southern California, 2005.

18. Robert Griffith, *The Politics of Fear: Joseph McCarthy and the Senate* (Amherst: University of Massachusetts Press, 1987), 262.

19. Griffith, *Politics of Fear*, 271.

20. David Petegorsky, "Our Civil Liberties in 1954," *Hadassah Newsletter*, November 1954, 1.

21. "In Defense of Democracy," speech script, call no. 3, box 18, folder 14, HA.

22. Howard Sachar, *The History of the Jews in America* (New York: Vintage Books, 1992), 622.

23. Sachar, *History of the Jews*, 622.

24. Ann Petluck, *Hadassah Newsletter*, December 1952, 2.

25. Petluck, 2.

26. Hubert Humphrey, "The Crisis in Liberalism," *Hadassah Newsletter*, March 1953, 2

27. Herbert H. Lehman, "For a Fair and Just Immigration Policy," *Hadassah Newsletter*, April 1954, 3.

28. Sachar, *History of the Jews*, 622.

29. Harry N. Rosenfeld, "Basic Issues in Immigration Policy," *Hadassah Newsletter*, March 1957, n.p.

30. Nancy J. Weiss, "Long Distance Runners of the Civil Rights Movement," in *Struggles in the Promised Land: Toward a History of Black–Jewish Relations in the United States*, Jack Salzman and Cornel West, eds. (Cambridge: Oxford University Press, 1997), 130.

31. Murray Friedman, *What Went Wrong: The Creation and Collapse of a Black–Jewish Alliance* (NY: The Free Press, 1995), 105.

31. Cheryl Greenberg, "Negotiating Coalition: Black and Jewish Civil Rights" in *Struggles in the Promised Land*, 160.

33. "Supreme Court Decision Banning Segregation," New York 1954, call no. 3, box 18, folder 8, HA.

34. Shirli Brautbar. "'Not Just Ladies That Lunch': Hadassah and the Formation of American Jewish Identity." PhD dissertation, University of Southern California, 2005.

35. Channing H. Tobias, "United We Stand: Supreme Court Ends School Segregation," *Hadassah Newsletter*, June 1954, 1.

36.   Tobias, "United We Stand," 1.

37.   Tobias, "United We Stand," 2.

38.   Tobias, "United We Stand," 2.

39.   "American Affairs Annual Report," September 1955–1956, 35, in box 19 folder 3, HA.

40.   John J. Gunther, "Civil Rights Act," *Hadassah Newsletter,* September 1957, n.p.; "Highlights of American Affairs-UN Activity," *Hadassah Headlines,* Dec 1957, 6.

41.   "Clippings 1958/59" scrapbook, HA.

42.   "Austin Yearbook," 1957, foreword, in call no. 15, box 17, HA.

43.   "Press Release," 22–23 October 1958, 3, call no. 3, box 19, folder 10, HA.

44.   "Press Release," 22–23 October 1958, 3, call no. 3, box 19, folder 10, HA.

45.   *Mount Vernon Chapter of Hadassah* 3, October 1956, 1.

46.   *Mount Vernon Chapter of Hadassah* 3, October 1956, 2.

47.   *Hadassah Shoreline* 3, no. 2, October 1956, 1, in call no. 15, box 5, "newsletter shoreline" folder, HA.

48.   "Press Release," 22–23 October 1958, 3, call no. 3, box 19, folder 10, HA

49.   Waldo E. Martin Jr., "Nation Time!" in *Struggles in the Promised Land,* ed. Jack Salzman and Cornel West (Oxford University Press, 1997), 343.

50.   Debra Schultz, *Going South: Jewish Women in the Civil Rights Movement* (New York University Press: New York, 2001).

51.   "Hadassah Annual Report 1960," 35, call no. 3, box 3, folder 6, HA; "American Affairs Annual Report July 1961–June 30 1962," 1, call no. 3, box 23, folder 7, HA; "American Affairs Annual Report July 1965–June 30 1966," 7, call no. 3, box 2, folder 4, HA; "Hadassah Annual Report," 1 July 1966 to 30 June 1967, 6, call no. 3, box 26, folder 6, HA.

52.   Anthony Lewis, "Civil Rights Report: The Momentum of History Is Working against Segregation," *Hadassah Newsletter,* January 1962, 3.

53.   Mrs. Louis Parris and Mrs. Benjamin Reed, "American Affairs," *Philadelphia Chapter News Bulletin,,* October 1951, n.p.

54.   Mrs. Norman Bram, "National Board Passes Resolutions Vital in National and World Peace," *Philadelphia Chapter Hadassah News Bulletin,* March 1961, n.p.

55.   *Hadassah Magazine,* April 1964, 9.

56.   *Hadassah Magazine,* April 1964, 22.

57.   Ruth Gruber Michaels, "March on Washington," *Hadassah Magazine,* September 1963, 40.

58.   Ruth Gruber Michaels, "March on Washington," *Hadassah Magazine,* September 1963, 40.

59.   "The Presidents Column," *Hadassah Magazine,* September 1963, 2.

60.   "Hadassah Resolutions," 1963, 2, box 23, folder 11, HA.

61.   "Press Release," 20 August 1964, 4, box 23, folder 11, HA.

62.   "American Affairs Kit," March-April 1965, AA-1, HA.

63.   "American Affairs Kit," AA-1, HA.

64.   "Civil Rights Act of 1966" as listed in "Annual Resolutions," August 1966, 2, in call no. 3, box 26, folder 5, HA.

65. Martin, "Nation Time," 346.

66. Martin, "Nation Time," 351,

67. "Black Power Can Be Helpful," *Hadassah Magazine,* Sept. 1968, n.p.; "Press Release: Special 1968 Convention Issue," 9, call no. 3, box 26, folder 5, HA.

68. "The Testament of Martin Luther King Jr.," *Hadassah Magazine,* May 1968, 8.

69. "The Testament of Martin Luther King Jr.," 8.

70. Robert Gordis piece, *Hadassah Magazine,* November 1968, 9.

71. "American Affairs Kit," 1 October 1968, AA-4, HA.

72. "American Affairs Kit," 17 February 1969, AA-6 to AA-9, HA.

73. "America Affairs Kit," April 1969, AA-2.5, HA.

74. "America Affairs Resolutions," October 1969, 2, call no. 3, box 28, folder 3, HA.

75. As quoted in William H. Chafe, *The Unfinished Journey: America Since World War II* (New York: Oxford University Press, 1995), 233.

76. "Press Release," 20 August 1964, 3, HA.

77. "American Affairs Annual Report," 2, call no. 3, box 26, folder 4, HA.

78. "American Affairs Anti-Poverty Legislation," September 1967, 2, HA.

79. "American Affairs Kit," 17 February 1969, HA; "American Affairs Kit," May–June 1965, HA; "American Affairs Kit," 15 April 1969, call no. 15, box 95, folder 1a, HA; "American Affairs Kit," 1 October 1968, HA; "American Affairs Kit," 15 December 1969, HA.

Chapter IV

1. Mary McCune, "Social Workers in the *Muskeljudentum*: 'Hadassah Ladies,' 'Manly Men' and the Significance of Gender in the American Zionist movement 1912-1928," *American Jewish History* 86, no. 2 (June 1998): 136–137

2. McCune, "Social Workers," 137–139; Michael Berkowitz, *Zionist Culture and West European Jewry Before the First World War* (Chapel Hill, University of North Carolina Press, 1993)

3. McCune, "Social Workers," 138-139.

4. McCune, "Social Workers," 138–139; June Sochen, *Consecrate Every Day: The Public Lives of Everyday Women* (Albany: State University of New York Press, 1981), 66.

5. Hasia R. Diner, *Her Works Praise Her: A History of Jewish Woman from Colonial Times to the Present* (New York: Basic Books, 2002), 110.

6. Charlotte Baum, Paula Hyman, and Sonya Michel, *The Jewish Woman in America* (New York: New American Library, 1975), 29; Diner, *Her Works,* 110; June Sochen, *Consecrate Every Day: The Public Lives of Everyday Women* (Albany: State University of New York Press, 1981), 10.

7. Hasia Diner, *A Time for Gathering: The Second Migration, 1820–1880*, vol. 2 of *The Jewish People in America* (Baltimore: John Hopkins University Press, 1992), 54, 56.

8. Diner, *Time for Gathering,* 1.

9. Diner, *Time for Gathering,* 64–66; Baum, Hyman, and Michel, *Jewish Woman,* 26.

10. Diner, *Time for Gathering*, 113.

11. Diner, *Her Works*, 110.

12. Diner, *Her Works*, 11.

13. Baum, Hyman, and Michel, *Jewish Woman*, 30; Diner, *Her Works*, 11.

14. Baum, Hyman, and Michel, *Jewish Woman*, 30; Diner, *Her Works*, 116.

15. Baum, Hyman, and Michel, *Jewish Woman*, 31.

16. Diner, *Her Works*, 121; Baum, Hyman, and Michel, *Jewish Woman*, 30.

17. Diner, *Her Works*, 125; Karla Goldman, *Beyond the Synagogue Gallery* (Cambridge: Harvard University Press: 2000).

18. Diner, *Her Works*, 121; Paula Hyman, *Gender and Assimilation in Modern Jewish History: The Roles and Representations of Women* (University of Washington Press, 1995).

19. Sochen, *Consecrate Every*, 45.

20. Hyman, *Gender and Assimilation*, 93.

21. Hyman, *Gender and Assimilation*, 100; Peiss, *Cheap Amusements: Working Women and Leisure in Turn-of-the-Century New York* (Philadelphia, Temple University Press, 1986); Nan Enstad, *Ladies of Labor Girls of Adventure: Working Women, Popular Culture, and Labor Politics at the Turn of the Twentieth Century* (New York: Columbia University Press,1999). Elizabeth Ewen, *Immigrant Women in the Land of Dollars* (New York: Monthly Review *Press, 1985).*

22. Sochen, *Consecrate Every*, 49.

23. Sochen, *Consecrate Every*, 48.

24. Faith Rogow, *Gone to Another Meeting* (Tuscaloosa: University of Alabama Press, 1993); Sochen, *Consecrate Every*, 2.

25. Rogow, *Gone*, 5.

26. Rogow, *Gone*, 5.

27. Rogow, *Gone*, 173.

28. Lichtenberg, "Hadassah's Founders," 18.

29. Sochen, *Consecrate Every*, 68.

30. Diner, *Her Works*, 313.

31. Karen Brodkin, *How Jews Became White Folks and What That Says about Race in America* (New Brunswick, NJ: Rutgers University Press, 1998).

32. Brodkin, *How Jews*, 41.

33. Brodkin, *How Jews*, 45; Diner, *Her Works*, 333.

34. Diner, *Her Works*, 371.

35. "This Is Your Life," brochure, 1954, 5, in call no. 17, box 8, "1950s" folder, Hadassah Archives (hereafter HA), Center for Jewish History, New York.

36. Hadassah, "On You It's Becoming," brochure, 1953, 4, in call 17, box 8, "1950s" folder, HA.

37. Hadassah, "Hadassah Makes You Important!" brochure, 3, in call no. 17, box 8, "1950s" folder, HA.

38. *Austin Yearbook*, 1948, 1 in call no. 15, folder 17, HA.

39. "Across the Country Wires," 7, call no. 15, box 13, "conferences 1954-1959" folder, HA.

40. Levin, *It Takes*, 172–173.

41. Hadassah, "On You It's Becoming," 8.

42. "Wanted a Mother," brochure, in scrapbook no. 4, HA.

43. "Wanted a Mother," brochure, in scrapbook no. 4, HA.

44. May.

45. "This Is Your Life," 8.

46. "It's Your Child Too," in-house ad, *Hadassah Newsletter*, October 1950, 4.

47. "This Is Your Life," 5.

48. "Hadassah Makes You Important," 3, and "Hadassah A Way of Life," 5, both in call no. 17, box 8, "1950s" folder, HA.

49. Hadassah, "On You It's Becoming," 5.

50. "Mrs. Rosensohn's address," speech, Opening Session Convention, 26 October 1952, 9, in call no. 3, box 17, folder 6, HA.

51. "Hands of Healing," *Hadassah Newsletter*, Jan 1951, 5.

52. Josselyn Shore, "My Career as a Hadassah Husband," *Hadassah Newsletter,* September 1953, 7.

53. Ibid.

54. Miriam Fierst and Lili Eller, "Who Is She? An Appraisal of the Composite of the Hadassah Member," *Hadassah Newsletter*, Oct 1958, 9.

55. Miriam Fierst and Lili Eller, "Who Is She?" 9.

56. Fierst and Eller, "Who Is She," 9.

Chapter V

1. "Press release October 22, 1958," call no. 3, box 19, folder 10, Hadassah Archives at the American Jewish Historical Society housed at the Center for Jewish History, New York, NY (hereafter HA).

2. "Press release October 22, 1958."

3. Betty Friedan, *The Feminine Mystique* (New York: Norton, 1963); Elaine Tyler May, *Homeward Bound: American Families on the Cold War* (New York: Basic Books, 1988); JoAnne Meyerowitz, *Not June Cleaver: Women and Gender in Postwar America, 1945–1960* (Philadelphia: Temple University Press, 1994); Nancy Walker, "Humor and Gender Roles: The 'Funny' Feminism of the Post–World War II Suburbs," *American Quarterly* 37 (1985): 98–113; Wini Breines, *Young White and Miserable: Growing Up Female in the Fifties* (Boston: Beacon Books, 1992); Jessamyn Nuehaus, "The Way to a Man's Heart: Gender Roles, Domestic Ideology, and Cookbooks in the 1950s," *Journal of Social History* (Spring 1999): 529–555; Susan Douglas, *Where the Girls Are: Growing Up Female with the Mass Media* (New York: Times Books, 1994); Lynn Spiegel, *Welcome to the Dream House: Popular Media and Postwar Suburbs* (Durham: Duke University Press, 2001).

4

5.   Jenna Weissman Joselit, *A Perfect Fit: Clothes, Character, and the Promise of America* (New York: Metropolitan Books, 2001), 25–27.

6.   Barbara A. Schreier, *Becoming American Women: Clothing and the Jewish Immigrant Experience, 1880–1920* (Chicago: Chicago Historical Society, 1994); Paula Hyman, *Gender and Assimilation* (Seattle: University of Washington Press, 1995); Elizabeth Ewen, *Immigrant Women in the Land of Dollars* (New York: Monthly Review Press, 1985).

7.   "Junior Hadassah to Stage Fashion Show," *Los Angeles Times*, 16 October 1932, sect. B, 18; "Clubwomen Today," 10 April 1934, sect. A, 7; "Along the Jersey Shore," *New York Times*, June 11, 1937, sect. 11, 2; "Club Meetings This Week," *New York Times*, 2 March 1941, sect. D, 5.

8.   Friedan, *Feminine Mystique*.

9.   Joanne Meyerowitz, "Beyond the Feminine Mystique: A Reassessment of Post-War Mass Culture, 1946–1958," in *Not June Cleaver; Women and Gender in Post-War America*, ed. Joanne Meyerowitz (Philadelphia: Temple University Press, 1994); Sylvie Murray, *The Progressive Housewife: Community Activism in Suburban Queens* (Philadelphia: University of Pennsylvania Press, 2003); Nancy Walker, "Humor and Gender Roles"; Breines, *Young White and Miserable*; Jessamyn Nuehaus, "The Way to a Man's Heart"; Douglas, *Where the Girls Are*; Spiegel, *Welcome to the Dream House*; Joyce Antler, "Between Culture and Politics: The Emma Lazarus Federation of Jewish Women's Clubs and the Promulgation of Women's History, 1944–1989," in *Unequal Sisters: A Multicultural Reader in U.S. Women's History*, ed. Vicki Ruiz and Ellen Carol Dubois, 3rd edition (New York: Routledge, 2000).

10. Anne Frior Scott, *Natural Allies: Women's Associations in American History* (Chicago: University of Illinois, 1991); Susan Levine, *Degrees of Equality* (Philadelphia: Temple University Press, 1995). For more on women's organizations, see also Ruth Bordin, *Women and Temperance: The Quest for Power and Liberty* (New Brunswick, NJ: Rutgers University Press, 1990); Kenneth D. Rose, *American Women and the Repeal of Prohibition* (New York: New York University Press, 1996); Caryn Neumann, "The End of Gender Solidarity: The History of the Women's Organization for National Prohibition Reform in the United States, 1929–1933," *Journal of Women's History* 19, no. 2 (Summer 1997): 31–51.

11. Margaret Finnegan, *Consumer Culture and Votes for Women* (New York: Columbia University Press, 1999), 3.

12. Finnegan, *Consumer Culture*, 21, 93.

13. Beverly Gordon, *Bazaars and Fair Ladies: The History of the American Fundraising Fair* (Knoxville: University of Tennessee Press, 1998), 5.

14. Matt Jacobson, *Whiteness of a Different Color: European Immigrants and the Alchemy of Race* (Cambridge, MA: Harvard University Press, 1999). On Father Coughlin's anti-Semitism, see Michael Kazin, *The Populist Persuasion: An American History* (Ithaca, NY: Cornell University Press, 1995), 109–134. On Henry Ford's anti-Semitism, see Neil Baldwin, *Henry Ford and the Jews: Mass Production of Hate* (Cambridge, MA: Perseus, 2003). On Smith, see Glen Jeansonne, *Gerald L. K. Smith: Minister of Hate* (New Haven, CT: Yale University Press, 1988).

15.	Karen Brodkin, *How Jews Became White Folks and What that Says about Race in America* (New Brunswick, NJ: Rutgers University Press, 1998), 142.

16.	Lois Banner, *American Beauty* (New York: Knopf, 1983), 14–15. For more books that detail the oppressive aspects of fashion and beauty culture consumption in history, see Joan Jacobs Brumberg, *The Body Project: An Intimate History of American Girls* (New York: Random House, 1997); Naomi Wolf, *The Beauty Myth* (New York: W. Morrow, 1991); Susan Bordo, *Unbearable Weight: Feminism, Western Culture, and the Body* (Berkeley: University of California Press, 1993).

17.	Kathy Peiss, *Cheap Amusements: Working Women and Leisure in Turn-of the-Century New York* (Philadelphia: Temple University Press, 1986); Nan Enstad, *Ladies of Labor Girls of Adventure: Working Women, Popular Culture, and Labor Politics at the Turn of the Twentieth Century* (New York: Columbia University Press,1999).

18.	Bordo, Unbearable Weight; Joan Jacobs Brumberg, Fasting Girls: The Emergence of Anorexia Nervosa as a Modern Disease (Cambridge, MA: Harvard University Press, 1988).

19.	This is not to suggest that it could not also be objectifying at the same time as it empowers.

20.	Alexandra Palmer, *Couture and Commerce: The Transatlantic Fashion Trade in the 1950s* (Vancouver: University of British Columbia Press, 2001), 128.

21.	Henrietta Szold (1941) as quoted in "Hadassah Annual Report 1952–1953: Vocational Education," call no. 3, box 17, folder 7, HA. This same quote is found on many official Hadassah reports and statements.

22.	"Israel Fashions Made by Seligsberg Graduates Are Delegates' Delight," *Hadassah Headlines*, December 1949, 6; press release 6, call no. 17, "Headlines" folder, HA; press release, 18 November 1949, 8, call no. 3, box 15, folder 4, HA.

23.	Press release, 18 November 1949, 8, HA.

24.	Julia Dushkin, "Fashions Flown From Israel," *Hadassah Newsletter,* September 1950, 8.

25.	Press release, 18 November 1949, 8; "Description of Eight of Fifteen Fashions Displayed at First Fashion Show of Israel Couture: Hadassah Convention, Monday Afternoon, Nov. 14 Fairmont Hotel," 1, in call no. 3, box 15, folder 4, HA.

26.	Quote directly from "Description of the Eight of Fifteen," 1–2. *Oriental* and *exotic* were terms used in Hadassah descriptive and promotional materials for the fashion shows.

27.	"Description of Eight of Fifteen," 1–2.

28.	"Description of Eight of Fifteen," 1–2.

29.	"Israel Fashions Made," 6; Press release, 6, call no. 17, "Headlines" folder, HA.

30.	"Across the Country Wires," 7, call no. 15, box 13, "conferences 1954–1959" folder, HA.

31.	"Fashion Show Help Youth Services Raise $600,000 Quota," *Hadassah Headlines*, n.d. 1950, 6.

32.	"Visual Aids Dramatize Vocational Education at Convention: Chapters May Now Order Them," *Hadassah Headlines*, December 1952, 5, HA.

33.	"Fashion Show Already Booked to the Hilt," *Hadassah Headlines*, January 1950, 5.

34. "Fashion Show Getting 'Rave' Notices," *Hadassah Headlines*, April 1952, 5.

35. Ibid.

36. Josselyn Shore, "My Career as a Hadassah Husband," *Hadassah Newsletter*, September 1953, 7.

37. Susan Douglas, *Where the Girls Are: Growing Up Female with the Mass Media* (New York: Basic Books, 1995), 50–55. Elaine Tyler May, *Homeward Bound: American Families in the Cold War Era* (New York: Basic Books, 1988).

38. "Fashion Show Getting 'Rave' Notices," *Hadassah Headlines*, April 1952, 5.

39. Image Mimosa; "Fashion Show Description of Dresses 1951," 1, call no. 18, Photograph Series, HA.

40. "Fashion Show Getting 'Rave Notices,'" 5.

41. "Hadassah Trains Airline Personnel," *Hadassah Newsletter*, September 1951, 6–7.

42. "Convention Report," *Hadassah Newsletter*, September 1954, 8.

43. Tim Brooks and Earle Marshall, *Complete Television Directing to Prime Time TV* (New York: Ballantine, 1999), 1012.

44. "Convention Report," 8.

45. Howard Sachar, *A History of Israel from the Rise of Zionism to Our Time* (New York: Alfred Knopf, 1996), 538.

46. Brodkin, How Jews Became White Folks; Jacobson, Whiteness.

47. "Patterns for Hadassah," *Hadassah Newsletter*, September 1951.

48. "Fashion Show Already Booked to the Hilt," *Hadassah Headlines*, January 1950, 5; Richard Martin and Harold Koda, *Orientalism: Visions of the East in Western Dress* (New York: The Metropolitan Museum of Art, 1994), and Edward Said, *Orientalism* (New York: Vintage Books, 1979). On the subject of Jews and Orientalism, see Ivan Kalmar and Derek Penslar, eds., *Orientalism and the Jews* (Waltham, MA: Brandeis University Press, 2005), and the special edition of *Shofar: An Interdisciplinary Journal of Jewish Studies* 24, no. 2 (Winter 2006).. Howard Sachar, *A History of Israel from the Rise of Zionism to Our Time* (New York: Alfred Knopf, 1996).

49. "Fashion Show Already Booked to the Hilt," *Hadassah Headlines*, January 1950, 5.

50. Elizabeth Ewing, *History of twentieth Century Fashion* (Hollywood: Costume and Fashion Press, 2001).

51. Caption on back of photo, RG 18, Photographs, HA.

52. *Women in Israel: Based on Material by Molly Lyons Bar-David* (New York: Education Department, Hadassah, 1952), 1.

53. *Women in Israel*, 2.

54. Friedan, *Feminine Mystique*; May, *Homeward Bound*; Brodkin, *How Jews Became White Folks*; Riv-Ellen Prell, *Fighting to Become Americans: Assimilation and the Trouble between Jewish Women and Jewish Men* (Boston: Beacon Press, 1999)

55. H. Y. Engel, "Shopping Bag Brigade Begins Membership Drive," *Hadassah Newsletter*, March 1952, n.p.

56. Ibid.

57. "ILGWU Cutters Preparing Garments for Hadassah," *Hadassah Newsletter*, September 1949, 6.

58. Westchester local bulletin in "Across the Country Wires," 7, no. call 15, box 13, "conferences 1954–1957" folder, HA.

59. "Keeping Time with Hadassah Westchester," call no. 15, box 13, "conferences 1954–1957" folder, HA.

60. "Keeping Time with Hadassah in Westchester," call no. 14, box 13, "conferences 1954–1959" folder, HA.

61. *Hadassah Shoreline*, Nov 1958, n.p. in call 15, box 5, HA; *Shoreline Newsletter*, December 1959, n.p., in call 15, box 5, HA.

62. "Convention Report," *Hadassah Magazine*, December 1963, 8.

63. "Secretary and Homemaker," *Hadassah Magazine*, June 1964, 1.

64. Mrs. Harry Donner, "From the President's Pen," *Philadelphia Chapter Hadassah News Bulletin*, September 1961, 1. All references to this bulletin stem from the periodical collection of the Philadelphia Historical Society (hereafter PHS).

65. "Peek Preview for 1960–1961: Master Kit Shows New 'Line' To Be Match for Paris High Style," *Hadassah Headlines*, June–July 1960, 2. All references to *Hadassah Headlines* from call no. 17, "Hadassah Headlines" folder, HA.

66. *Hadassah Headlines*, May 1960, 2.

67. "Chapters Swing into H-Month Campaigns with Member-Getting Gimmicks, Ideas, and Incentives," *Hadassah Headlines*, September–October 1962, 1.

68. "Filmed Fashion Show Is Fine Forerunner: Fund-Raising Pitch for Vocational Education," *Hadassah Headlines*, November 1962.

69. Interview with Mrs. Morris Kertzer, "H######igher Hems Can Mean Higher Supplies Total," *Hadassah Headlines*, June–July 1966, 4.

70. "Filmed Fashion Show," 6.

71. W. Granger Blair, "Israel Seeks a Place in the Fashion World," *Hadassah Magazine*, April 1965, 12; Ruth Gruber Michaels, "Israel Fashions in USA," *Hadassah Magazine*, Oct 1966, 8; Ruth Gruber Michaels, "Israel's Fashion Mission," *Hadassah Magazine*, April 1967, 12.

Chapter VI

1. "Mrs. Jacobson Calls for Arab Talks," *Hadassah Newsletter*, September 1968, n.p.

2. "Convention 1960," New York, 8, call no. 3, box 21, folder 6, HA.

3. "Convention 1962 Press Release," 19 September 1962, 2, call no. 3, box 23, folder 6, HA.

4. Resolution, August 1965 convention, 27, call no. 3, box 25, folder 4, HA.

5. "Annual Conference," October 1963, 3, call no. 3, box 23, folder 11, HA.

6. "Resolutions Adopted," Los Angeles 1964, 25, HA.

7. "Resolutions Adopted," Los Angeles, 1964.

8. Resolutions, February 1965, call no. 15, "Zionist Affairs circulation" folder, circulation material 1965, HA.

9. Resolutions, February 1965.

10. Resolutions, convention August 1966, 27 call no. 3, box 26, folder 5, HA.

11. "Convention 1965, mid-winter, February, Zionist Affairs Arab Aggression," call no. 15, "Zionist Affairs" circulation folder, HA.

12. "August 1965 Resolutions," 27, call no. 3, box 25, folder 4, HA.

13. Resolutions, convention 1966, 27, call no. 3, box 26, folder 5, HA; Judy Heller, "President's Message," *Hadassah Bulletin Chaim Weizman Chapter*, October 1967, 1.

14. Press release, convention 1962, 19 September 1962, 1, call no. 3, box 23, folder 6, HA.

15. Resolutions, August 1965 annual convention, 6, call no. 3, box 25, folder4, HA; Resolutions, August 1966, 27, call no. 3, box 26, folder 5, HA.

16. "Convention Urges U.S. Adoption of Seven-Point Middle East Program," 21, call no. 3, box 21, folder 5, HA.

17. "Convention Urges U.S.," 21.

18. "Convention Urges U.S.," 21.

19. Golda Meir, "It's Never Too Late to Talk," *Hadassah Magazine*, November 1963, n.p.

20. For more on AIPAC, see Marla Brettschneider, *Cornerstones of Peace: Jewish Identity Politics and Democratic Theory* (New Brunswick, NJ: Rutgers, 1996).

21. "Zionist Affairs Annual Report," 1 July 1961 to 30 June 1962, call no. 3, box 23, folder 7, HA.

22. Letter from Miriam Freund, 10 May 1963, call no. 15, "Zionist Affairs" folder, circulated material, HA.

23. Resolution adopted at National Policy Conference of AIPAC, May 1963, circulated in "Zionist Affairs Kit," call no. 15 , "Zionist Affairs circulation" box, HA; "Zionist Affairs," letter, circulated 23 December 1963, call no. 15, "Zionist affairs circulation" box, HA; "Zionist Affairs Kit," 5 November 1964, call no. 15, Zionist affairs box, HA; "Zionist Affairs Kit," January 1965, call no. 15, "Zionist Affairs circulation" box, HA; "Zionist Affairs Kit," 1 February 1965, call no. 15, Zionist affairs box, HA; "Zionist Affairs Kit," 15 February 1965, box 15, HA.

24. "World Report: Jerusalem Awaiting Phantom Jets," *Hadassah Magazine*, January 1969, n.p.

25. "World Report: Jerusalem Awaiting Phantom Jets," n.p.

26. "World Report: Jerusalem Awaiting Phantom Jets," n.p.

27. "Emergency Act Now," advertisement, *Hadassah Headlines*, June 1967, 1.

28. Ruth Gruber Michaels, "Diary of an American Housewife; Support for Israel is Overwhelming," *Hadassah Newsletter*, special issue June 1967.

29. Edith Zamost, Oral History published in *A Tapestry of Hadassah Memories*. Miriam Freund Rosenthal, ed. (The Town House Press, 1994), 157.

30. Elie Wiesel, Article No Title, *Hadassah Newsletter*, special issue July 1967, 4.

31. Elie Wiesel, *Hadassah Newsletter*, special issue July 1967, 4.

32. Wiesel, 4.

33. Hadassah, "Zionist Affairs Kit," July 18, 1967, 1, call no. 15, Zionist affairs box, HA.

34. Hadassah, "Zionist Affairs Kit," July 18, 1967, 2.

35. Section titled "Israel Not an Arab land," in Hadassah, "Zionist Affairs Basic Information Kit," 1, call no. 15, Zionist Affairs Committee box, HA.

36. "Israel Not an Arab land" section, in Hadassah, "Zionist Affairs Basic Information Kit," 3.

37. Mrs. Theodore Cook, "The Israeli Scene," in *Philadelphia Chapter Hadassah Newsletter*, September 1960, 7.

38. Mrs. William Bass, "Zionist Affairs," *Philadelphia Chapter Hadassah News Bulletin*, October 1968, 3.

39. Ilan Pappe, *A History of Modern Palestine: One Land, Two Peoples* (Cambridge, UK: Cambridge University Press, 2004).

40. Pappe, *A History*, 149.

41. Pappe, *A History*, 196.

42. Resolutions, 1960 Annual Conference, 8, call no. 3, box 21, folder 6, HA.

43. Resolutions, August 1966 Conference, 26, call no. 3, box 26, folder 5, HA.

44. "Zionist Affairs Kit," November 1964, call no. 15, "Zionist Affairs Kit" box, "circulated material" folder, HA.

45. "Zionist Affairs Kit," November 1964, call no. 15, "Zionist Affairs Kit" box, "circulated material" folder, HA.

46. "Zionist Affairs Kit," November 1964.

47. "Zionist Affairs Kit," November 1964.

48. Mrs. Theodore Cook and Mrs. Louis Paris, "Hussein Travels with Arab Story" *Philadelphia Chapter Hadassah News Bulletin*, December 1967, 10.

49. Cook and Paris, "Hussein Travels with Arab," 10.

50. Clipping, *Congressional Record,* 23 January 1967, call no. 15, "Congressional records" folder, HA.

51. "Security Yes, Peace No: One Year After the Six Day War," *Hadassah Magazine*, June 1968, n.p.

52. Rubinstein, "Hadassah Magazine: World Report," 2.

53. "Our Vocational Program Also Created Programs to Meet and Know Arabs of Israel," *Hadassah Headlines*, June 1962, 6.

54. "Position of Arabs in Israel," *Hadassah Headlines*, No Date, 4, 7.

55. Phillip Gillion, "Arabs Come to Ein Karen," *Hadassah Magazine*, January 1969, n.p.

56. Rose Carlin, "Little Nasser at the Medical Center," *Hadassah Magazine*, March 1964, 34.

57. "Our Medical Role within Unified Jerusalem has International Import," *Hadassah Magazine,* October 1967, 3.

58. Gillion "Arabs Come," n.p.

59. Molly Bar-David, "Diary of an Israel Housewife," *Hadassah Magazine*, October 1967 25.

60. Bar-David, "Diary of an Israel Housewife," 25.

61. "Mrs. Samuel Halprin Takes Issue with Premier Ben Gurion on Role of Zionist Movement Today," box 21, folder 5, HA.

62. "Mrs. Samuel Halprin Takes Issue."

63. "Mrs. Samuel Halprin Takes Issue."

64. "Mrs. Samuel Halprin Takes Issue," 4.

65. Letter to Zionist Affairs chairman, 12 April 1965, call no. 15, "Zionist Affairs" box, "civic material 1965" folder, HA; "Zionist Affairs Issues Kit for Briefings, Study Course," *Hadassah Headlines*, June 1965, 4; "Zionist Affairs Chairman Urges Chapters to Utilize Updated High School Briefing Kits," *Hadassah Headlines*, May 1967, as compiled in call no. 17, "Headlines" folder, HA.

66. "Chapters Disseminate Factual Data on Israel to the Community," *Hadassah Headlines*, November 1964, 2.

67. "Hadassah Medical Organization Annual Report," Oct 1959-August 1960, 36–37, call no. 3, folder 6, HA; "Annual Reports; American Affairs Annual Report," July 1966-June 30, 3, call no. 3, box 26 folder 6, HA; American Affairs Kit, October 1 1968, "United Nations Course" American Affairs Kit, December 1968, last page, HA.

68. Resolutions, 1960 New York, 6, call no. 3, box 21, folder 6, HA.

69. "American Affairs UN Annual Report," 1, 2, call no. 3, box 23, folder 7, HA.

70. American Affairs Kit, January 1966, AA8, HA.

71. American Affairs Kit, January 1966, AA8.

72. American Affairs Kit, May-June 1966, aa-13, HA.

73. Resolutions, Boston, August 1966, 5, call no. 3, box 26, folder 5, HA. September 1967, 4.

74. Hadassah Annual Report, 1966–1967, 3, call no. 3, box 26, folder 6, HA.

75. "American Affairs Annual Report," July 1966–June 30, 3, call no. 3, box 26, folder 6, HA.

76. Press release, 17 Aug 1964, 4, HA.

77. Press release, 17 Aug 1964, 4.

78. Press release, 17 Aug 1964, 4.

79. Press release, 17 Aug 1964, 4.

80. Resolutions, Los Angeles national convention 1964, 26, HA.

81. Resolutions, Los Angeles national convention 1964, 26. HA.

82. Press release, 16 August 1965, HA.

83. Resolutions, Boston convention 1966, 28, call no. 3, box 26, folder 5, HA.

84. "Hadassah Medical Organization Annual Report," August 1960 1, no. 3, box 21, folder 6, HA.

INDEX

CPSIA information can be obtained at www.ICGtesting.com
Printed in the USA
LVOW10s2017180915

454785LV00004B/88/P

9 781618 112958